Cave of the Oracle

(1916)

L. W. de Laurence

ISBN 0-7661-0732-9

Kessinger Publishing's
Rare Mystical Reprints

THOUSANDS OF SCARCE BOOKS
ON THESE AND OTHER SUBJECTS:

Freemasonry * Akashic * Alchemy * Alternative Health * Ancient Civilizations * Anthroposophy * Astrology * Astronomy * Aura * Bible Study * Cabalah * Cartomancy * Chakras * Clairvoyance * Comparative Religions * Divination * Druids * Eastern Thought * Egyptology * Esoterism * Essenes * Etheric * ESP * Gnosticism * Great White Brotherhood * Hermetics * Kabalah * Karma * Knights Templar * Kundalini * Magic * Meditation * Mediumship * Mesmerism * Metaphysics * Mithraism * Mystery Schools * Mysticism * Mythology * Numerology * Occultism * Palmistry * Pantheism * Parapsychology * Philosophy * Prosperity * Psychokinesis * Psychology * Pyramids * Qabalah * Reincarnation * Rosicrucian * Sacred Geometry * Secret Rituals * Secret Societies * Spiritism * Symbolism * Tarot * Telepathy * Theosophy * Transcendentalism * Upanishads * Vedanta * Wisdom * Yoga * *Plus Much More!*

DOWNLOAD A FREE CATALOG AT:
www.kessinger.net

OR EMAIL US AT:
books@kessinger.net

The Cave Of The Oracle

The Cave Of The Oracle

THE GREAT WHITE BROTHERHOOD

Persian And Chaldean Magic

TALISMANIC MAGIC. OCCULTISM. SEALS AND TALISMANS; THEIR CONSTRUCTION, POWERS AND INFLUENCE. DREAMS, VISIONS, OMENS AND ORACLES. HEALING. TELEPATHY, CLAIRVOYANCE, SPIRITISM, AND BIBLE CONTRADICTIONS.

By
Dr. L. W. de Laurence

Author Of The Great Book Of Magical Art, Hindu Magic And East Indian Occultism. The Master Key. The Sacred Book Of Death And Hindu Spiritism. The Mystic Test Book Of The Hindu Occult Chambers. The Wonders Of The Magic Mirror. Crystal Gazing And Clairvoyance. Astral Auras And Colors. The Immanence Of God, Know Thyself. God, The Bible, Truth And Christian Theology. Medical Hypnosis And Magnetic Hypnotism. Manual Of Disease And Modern Medicine. Valmondi; The Old Book Of Ancient Mysteries. The Dead Man's Home, Etc., Etc.

de Laurence, Scott & Co.

Chicago, Ill., U. S. A.

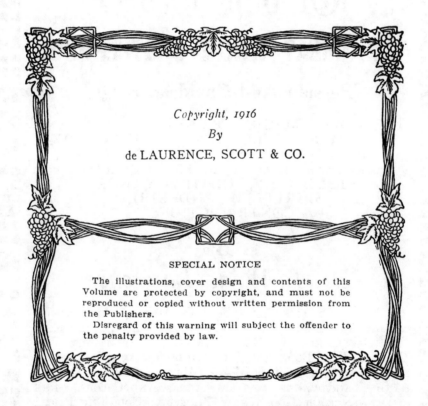

Copyright, 1916

By

de LAURENCE, SCOTT & CO.

SPECIAL NOTICE

The illustrations, cover design and contents of this Volume are protected by copyright, and must not be reproduced or copied without written permission from the Publishers.

Disregard of this warning will subject the offender to the penalty provided by law.

NOTICE—This work is protected by Copyright, and simultaneous initial publications in United States of America, Great Britain, France, Germany, Russia, India, China and other countries. All rights reserved.

Preface

It is not my intention in these pages to attempt an exposition of the deeper *arcana* in connection with the various subjects treated of; but rather to place before the lay reader a number of methods by means of which he will be able to demonstrate to his own satisfaction, and that of others, that there is a deep substratum of truth in what is usually called "Occultism," and that *Talismanic Magic* is a sure and definite means of exploring them.

The ancient *Hermetic* philosophers were well aware of a certain subtile correspondence or analogy existing between the superior and inferior worlds, the world of causation and that of effects. They traced a connection between the noumenal and the phenomenal, between the mind of man and his bodily condition, between the spiritual and the natural. They affirmed all this in a trite axiom: *As above, so below.* This philosophy extended to concrete observations, and became a science which they embodied in the Doctrine of Correspondences. The hieroglyphic writings of the *Hindus, Chinese, Egyptians* and *Assyrians* are the outcome of this science, portions of which are current in our own thought and language. Thus when we speak of commerce, the merchant and the market, we are going back to traditional knowledge which associated the *"winged messenger"* of the gods with the ship in full sail; the word *merx* (trade) being at the root of the name *Mercury,* and the symbol ☿ the hieroglyph for all that the name imports. We call the Sun *"he"* and the Moon *"she,"* tracing unconsciously a subtile correspondence between the day and the active male function in nature, and between the night and the passive female function. We speak of jovial men and infer their connection with the planet *Jupiter;* and all our destructive and hurtful ideas are embodied in such words as *"to mar," "martial," "murder,"* etc., linking them to their source in the root *marna* (to strike), because the destructive element in nature is represented in our system by the planet Mars.

This *Doctrine of Correspondences* is at the root of all *Occult* interpretation. It is our human presentation of the Universal Law which binds the *Microcosm* to the *Macrocosm* as an effect to its antecedent cause. The mystic, the poet and the creative artist are all unconscious interpreters of this universal law. They have in some degree the universal sense by which their souls are rendered responsive to the pulsations of *Nature's* own heartbeat. The *sybil*, the *diviner* and the *seer* are in even closer touch with the Great Life, while they have less conscious enjoyment of that intimacy. Others there are who reach to the heart of things by a clear and conscious intellection, understanding what they see, analyzing and interpreting what they feel. These are the Adepts of India, the true masters of the secret knowledge. Here it is perhaps necessary to mark the distinction which exists between Adeptship and mediumism, between the voluntary conscious effort of the trained intellect and the automatic functioning of the natural "sensitive," in their respective relations to the *occult* world.

The Adept is one who intelligently and continuously applies himself to the understanding of the hidden forces in nature and to the laws of the interior world, to the end that he may consciously co-operate with nature and the spiritual intelligences in the production of effects of service to himself and to his fellow-beings. This entails upon him a close study of the mystery and

PREFACE

power of *sound, number, color, form;* the *Occult* laws underlying all expression of faculty; the laws of *sympathy* and *antipathy;* the law of *vibration;* of *spiritual* and *natural* affinity; the law of *periodicity,* of *cosmic energy, planetary action;* occult correspondences, etc. To these labors he must bring a natural gift of understanding, an unusual degree of patience and devotion, and a keen perception of natural facts. The Medium, or natural sensitive, is one who holds himself in negative relations to the interior worlds, and submits himself to the operation of influences proceeding from things and persons, as well as to that of discarnate intelligences. The medium cultivates an unusual degree of responsiveness to environment and to the emanations (*atomic, magnetic or psychic*) and suggestions of other persons. The phenomena developed by this process of mediumism include *automatism* (temporary loss of control over the motor nerves), as in the phenomena of involuntary speech and automatic writing; *hyperæsthesia,* as in the function of clairvoyance, clairaudience, psychometry, etc.; *trance,* with its attendant phenomena of unconscious cerebration, obsession, and a variety of physical effects of a supernormal character. In its highest manifestation, following upon the "crucifying of the flesh," the subjugation of the passions, and a process of intense religious aspiration, mediumism is frequently followed by spiritual revelation and spontaneous prophecy. *"But this sort cometh not but by fasting and prayer."*

The various forms of *divination* to which recourse is had in so-called *occult* circles rest largely upon the exercise of a faculty which is compounded of *occultism* and *mediumism.* They are seen to employ the automatic faculty in conjunction with an empirical knowledge of certain *occult* methods of interpretation.

The following pages are intended to place the earnest student in possession of some of the principal methods of the Adepts and mediums. In this book will be found everything necessary to an initial understanding and practice of the various *occult* arts. It is within the author's purpose to place so much information at the disposal of the student as will effectually debar him from any excuse of ignorance concerning the *Occult* powers latent in man and the verity of *Talismanic Magic*. It is within the power of everybody to be convinced, and to convince others, while he who perseveres to the point of perfection in the exercise of his faculty may justly be dignified by the name of *Adept*. The *Magi* of ancient times were *astrologers, diviners* and *prophets* all, and he who would aspire to their high degree must pursue their methods and live their life. I will give below the following maxims, which are still preserved in the *Sacred Orders of The East;* of which I have the honor of being a member. They are: Know—Will—Dare—Keep Silent; and as to the rule of life they enjoin—Right Thought—Right Feeling—Right Speech—Right Action—Right Living.

Dr. L. W. de Laurence.

The Cave Of The Oracle

CHAPTER I

OCCULTISM AND TALISMANIC MAGIC

THE GREAT WHITE BROTHERHOOD

Before one can enter intelligently into an understanding of *Cosmic Symbolism*, which underlies all phases of *Talismanic Magic*, it is necessary that he should have some well-defined conception of the meaning and purpose of *Occultism*. Otherwise he will occupy the position of one who moves in the dark, a slave to formularies and dogmas, following blindly where others lead and without any definite idea as to his destination.

Misconceptions regarding *Occultism* and *Magic* are very prevalent and are found to affect the thought of many who in their own walks are exceedingly learned. *Occultism* is a broad and comprehensive system of thought; a synthetic philosophy aiming at *self-realization,* and as much concerned in the practical development of the psychical and spiritual powers latent in man as in the study of those wider cosmical laws which hitherto have escaped scientific observation, but which are found to afford a ready explanation of man's embodied existence, and the wide and varied range of his faculties, aptitudes and individual characteristics.

If *Occultism* were merely a speculative system of thought regarding the hidden powers of *Nature*, it could never find practical demonstration. If the *occult* were merely the *"hidden,"* then *Röntgen* rays, wireless telegraphy and metabolism would have been facts of *Occultism* at quite a recent date. In the first case it is confidently affirmed that *Occultism*, so far from being speculative, is capable of instant demonstration; and in the second case it anticipated the discoveries of Science by analogous psychical processes involved in the exercise of *clairvoyance, psychometry, telepathy* and *hypnotism*. True *Occultism* is not indeed mainly concerned in the domain of physics, but rather in those immaterial forces which are at the back of all material forms, of those universal laws which find their reflection in the constitution and development of man and the *cosmos* to which he is immediately related.

Thus while it demonstrates some unexplored facts in *Nature*, it also offers a coherent system of thought in which those facts find appropriate places, and so in effect it affords an ethical basis for all action which is more comprehensive than any system which is the outcome of an insular sociology or a national religion. Its peculiar value as a body of teaching lies in its *inclusiveness* and *catholicity*, its freedom from dogma, and its wide suggestiveness. While offering a definite system of *cosmogenesis* and *anthropogenesis*, it seeks only to throw new light on old truths, being entirely constructive and in no sense controversial. Unlike orthodox Science and Religion, however, *Occultism* does not ignore the facts of man's psychic and spiritual experience. Rather it makes use of these as links which bring us into relations with that greater world and that higher life for which Science has no interest and for Religion no certain meaning. Thus when Science repudiated the *Chaldean* account of the *Genesis*, Religion was left with no ground upon which it could convict

Science of error! The *Occultist* remains wholly unaffected by the incident, not because he is either unscientific or irreligious, but because the *Book of Genesis* is for him as true to-day as when it was written. It is the work of *Occultists,* and only *Occultists* can rightly apprehend it.

In the biblical *cosmogenesis* we are not concerned with ordinary divisions of time called *"day"* and *"night,"* periods of twelve hours each, more or less, but with vast periods known as *pralayas* and *manvantaras,* or periods of manifestation and obscuration, taking place alternately. These great periods answer to the systole and diastole motion of the *Great Breath,* the out-breathing and in-breathing of the *Cosmic Life-force.* In each of these great out-breathings the seven stages of evolution are realized: the *Igneous, Gaseous, Fluidic, Mineral, Vegetable, Animal* and *Human.* But those monads that have reached any one of these stages do not become involved in the scheme until that stage is reached to which they attained in the last period of cosmic activity; but from that stage they resume their evolution.

Now as we have every reason to presume that our present period of activity is not the first of our solar system, we have reason to place a special meaning on the words *Berâsit brâ Elohim âth hashemâyim veâth heâretz:* In the beginning the *Elohim* compounded the original matter of the heavens and of the earth. Long periods of cosmic evolution elapsed, and at the point where the *Great Breath* again reached our planet we take up the thread of the *Chaldean* account *veheâretz tohu vebohu: "and the earth was chaotic and barren."* The use of the prefix *vau* as a copulative conjunction at the beginning of each separate statement, links up the various stages of the evolutional scheme without defining the vast ages, the *"days"* and *"nights"* of the cosmos, which intervene. From the great aqueous development we pass to the amphibians, the *"creeping things,"* the avians or *"flying things and fowls of the air,"* until by a process of natural evolution and natural selection, determined entirely by the individual power of adaptation to environment, we at length arrive at the evolution of the human-animal. The brief but perfectly scientific statement, *"And God (the Elohim) made men out of the dust of the earth,"* is a process which involves an indefinitely long period of evolution.

But so far we have only the ascending arc of physical evolution, which in effect found its apotheosis in the production of giant human forms, fitted to the great struggle for existence with the *saurians* and *pachyderms* and all that mammoth life, both vegetable and animal, by which it was environed. "There were giants in the earth in those days." *Nature* had done her utmost in the production of colossal forms of animal life, she had expended all her strength.

It was at this point, where *Nature* unaided would have failed, and in process of time died down to her root, as a tree that has put forth leaf and flower and fruit, that the upward arc of *physical evolution* was met by a downward arc of *spiritual involution*. The two processes are well defined: 1. *God made man out of the dust of the earth.* 2. *And breathed into his nostrils the breath of lives.*

In effect, from this union of spirit and matter we get the genesis of the psyche or soul: *"and man became a living soul."* The process of becoming is one that was neither immediate nor complete. Most of us are still in the process of becoming. But a certain number of advanced *monads* became living souls, realizing their spiritual consciousness while in the flesh. These were the *"sons of the gods"* referred to in the text. All else were the sons of men. *"And the sons of God looked upon the daughters of men and saw that they*

were fair." The self-conscious souls took to wife the daughters of a less-evolved race, a process that would seem to be necessary to the further uplifting and spiritual vitalizing of the inferior grades of human life. During the present *manvantara* or period of *cosmic* activity we have traditional *occult* knowledge of four great races of humanity before our own, each of which attained to a successively higher state of civilization, the *Atlantean* transcending the *Lemurian,* as in process of time the *Aryan* will transcend the *Atlantean.* And as each period of *cosmic* activity has afforded means of successively higher human development, it is a question as to what has become of those very high forms of spiritualized humanity who were the final product of the material and spiritual evolution of past *manvantaras.* Earth-born in their origin, and linked to this Earth's humanity by a thousand compatriot ties, by bonds of blood and heritage, by lives of tireless service, they wait the time when humanity shall have evolved to that stage when personal intercourse is compatible with their own spiritual status and the needs of our further evolution. To them, as pioneers, guardians or masters of the race, we are indebted for the universal tradition which here and there is gathered up by *Occultists* the world over, and which is realized in its integrity only by those who have fought their way to that place in the scale of spiritual evolution where detachment is possible. To them is attributable the founding of the great world religions, and at the outset these *"Sons of God"* were the spiritual instructors of the world. Each race produces its own masters, evolved initiates sworn to the service of man for ever. As there is a natural selection, so there is a spiritual selection, and from the moment a human form is invested with a soul (psyche) that soul continues to pro-
 ss. There is an evolution that has come along the natural line to the production of human lives of great

faculty and attainment; and there is an evolution that has followed the spiritual line. Not all evolved humans are invested with the breath of *lives*. Thus a man may be an intellectual giant and yet not be ensouled, for the *psyche* is one thing and the *pneuma* is another. The *psyche* or *nephesh* is common to man and the lower animals and is capable of immense development when investing the human form, but unless this *nephesh* is illuminated by the *ruach* or *pneuma* it cannot advance beyond a certain stage in the present cycle of evolution. Hence the saying, *"Work while the day is yet with you, for the night cometh when no man shall work."*

Specialized humanity is a composite of spirit, mind, soul and body. The element or principle in man which distinguishes him from the animal (whether human in form or otherwise), is the *Mind*. *Only* in this possession is he truly man. The word man comes, indeed, from the root *man* (Sansk.), to think. The limitations set up by embodiment of this thinking self is the primary cause of self-realization. All forms of life are conscious, but only spiritualized humanity is self-conscious, or individualized.

The criterion of consciousness is response to stimulus. It is to be seen in chemic action, in vegetation and in animal life. If the Day's-eye (daisy) were not conscious of the sunrise it would not open its petals. You may call it automatism, a reflex of the chemic action of light. You will be wiser if you call it consciousness of light, and so spare yourself the trouble of pushing the question back indefinitely, for somewhere or other you must admit response to stimulus and there you must posit consciousness.

Thus while the animal soul in man responds to stimulus of every kind coming to it through the sense-channels, the mind responds also to a higher and immaterial gamut of vibrations, that is to say, to spiritual stimulus. As man he continues to evolve while all other forms of life remain in *statu quo*. The *monads* investing them have not been caught up by the Oversoul; they have not reached the stage where their *mass-vibration* is capable of responding to the spiritual impact; they are not attracted.

As the outcome of human evolution through successive ages, cycles and manvantaras there is evolved the *Christ* or perfect man. The mystical interpretation does not suffice. We require a living individual who shall stand to us for the "man made perfect" through that same process of spiritual evolution which is to be our own means of final liberation from *samsara*, or cyclic rebirth. The *Christ* is truly a generic title. The sons of God are legion, and all of them are invested with the Spirit of Truth or *Christ* principle. They are the *Children of Light*, the *Great White Brotherhood*, and at their head is the Lord, the gravitating Centre of this world's humanity. He is the manifestation in time and space of the inscrutible *Deity*, the revelation of God to man. The mythological interpretation of the *Christ* does not suffice any more than the mystical. The *Sun* and the twelve signs of the *Zodiac* may well stand as symbols of the *Master* and his *twelve disciples*, but they will not suffice for the historical fact, for the fact is not limited to a drama in which thirteen characters were at one time employed. It is a drama that is playing through all time, in all places and among all peoples. It is the great work of spiritual selection and co-ordination, and the twelve signs are the twelve gates through which the elect of all humanity will enter into the *New Jerusalem* or Spiritual Kingdom of a perfected humanity. Neither is the kingdom one that is afar off. Its denizens are to be found among embodied humanity at this day. The Fathers and many of the early rulers of the great countries were special representatives of the *Spiritual Hierarchy* which at later stages in the history of the world sent forth its emissaries to become world-teachers, empire-makers, legislators, warriors and inventors, each speaking the Word that the world then had need of. Beside them are to be found the *Occultists* of the East and West, followers of their respective *Gurus, Sadhus, Yogis* and *Teachers,* aspirants to the heirloom of the ages, the *Gupta-Vidya* or *Hidden Knowledge;* with here and there a messenger under sealed orders, passing from one country to another; a host of psychic-researchers and higher-thought lecturers, the *aide-de-camps,* sappers and enlisting officers of the vast army of recruits, regulars and veterans who are enrolled under this standard.

To the *Occultist* the universe is a symbol and every part of it is symbolical. Although essentially an Idealist he does not attempt the rôle of those visionaries who would argue the universe out of existence. He may call it elusive but not an illusion, for his own existence depends on his consciousness of the world about him and his well-being upon the degree to which he understands and observes the laws of that universe of which he is an integral part. For if it be said that the world has no existence apart from our consciousness, it may with equal truth be said that our consciousness has no existence apart from the world to which it is related. What we understand as the laws of the universe are formulated in terms of our thought, but inasmuch as the laws of thought are imposed on us by existence, it is clear that we do not ourselves impose cosmic laws, but we merely apprehend them. It is not in the Idealistic sense that the universe is a symbol, but in the real sense of it being the embodiment or out-realizing of the *Supreme Life* and *Mind.* As symbol the universe is the revelation of all time, of the past and the future; the repository of all history, the source of all prophecy, the synthesis of actuality. That Consciousness which is simultaneously immanent in all the universe is called the *Universal Mind*. The Platonic definition of God as *"That whose centre is everywhere and whose circumference is illimitable"* comes as nearly to this conception of the *Divine Mind* as it is possible for words to compass. Man is a centre of consciousness in the *Divine Mind* from the time that he realizes his spiritual existence, a soul investing a cell in the Brain of the *Grand Man*. As such he becomes subject to the higher spiritual laws of Being and enters into the Divine Conspiracy. The evolving monads circulate and finally become impounded in one or another of the various organs of the *Grand Man*, in agreement with their several states of evolution, passing from one to another of them during the successive incarnations of the Deity. In his effort to reach a higher sphere of consciousness and activity, a wider sphere of influence and a greater measure of free will, man comes to realize that obedience to the law of his being is the means of attainment. Thus every man is a law unto himself, and the truly wise are they who are able to say in all consciousness: "Thy will be done." For human safety and happiness are only assured by devotion to the highest good, and this is the occult view of the dependence of mankind on an all-seeing and beneficent Spirit "in whose service is perfect freedom."

Occultism, therefore, whether consisting in the development and exercise of one's individual psychic powers, in systematic and impartial inquiry as to evidence of these powers in others, or in the pursuit of uch studies as *Astrology, Kabalism, Yoga, Hypnotism*, etc., reaches out from such vague beginnings into regions of thought and aspiration that transcend the average mind and are seen to culminate, in specialized cases, in the attainment of powers which may be called miraculous and of attributes that are truly godlike.

HINDU, PERSIAN AND CHALDEAN MAGIC

Magic is an art, or rather an unseen power, by means of which man attempts to avail himself of the *Occult* forces around him for the benefit of himself and his fellow beings. It is thus worthy of an important position in the history of the human mind. This science, as its name indicates, originated with the *Hindus, Egyptian,* and the *Persian Magi.* At different periods we find it occupying a field connected with that of religion. It is an application, a natural operation, so to speak, of our mental faculty; it is the realization of the popular axiom: *"If one doesn't believe in God, he must believe in himself."* We thus find spiritual beings divided into two distinct classes, the spirits of light and the spirits of darkness; into beneficent divinities, good and bad. It approaches religion in so far as it implies a belief in an invisible world, which it peoples with spirits superior to man. It also teaches that certain *Magical* practices possess the virtue of subduing such spirits to the will of man.

Magic has given rise to the use of *Philters, Talismans, Charms* and Seals, which are held to be capable of inspiring love or some other passion; some of them were for the purpose of causing jealousy, invulnerability and hatred. It would take too long to enumerate all of these *Talismans, Charms* and *Philters;* I shall later give some of the proceedings employed by the *Magician.*

* * * * * * *

Temple Incense is always used to evoke spirits and souls of the departed (have we not those who believe in spirits still, even in the twentieth century?); it causes *"geni"* to appear, mysterious words are spoken to them for the purpose of attracting both the good and the evil spirits.

As man's ideas in regard to the spiritual world become more exalted, *Magic* tends to become of a higher type: the word *Magic* alone arouses a man's faith in the Occult powers of *Nature*.

In order to write the history of *Magic*, it is necessary to go back to the most remote times. Examples of *Magic* are found in the Bible. *Cassien* attributes its invention to *Ham;* as he was unable to take with him into the ark the books treating of the subject, he engraved its principal dogmas on very hard materials capable of withstanding the action of the waters, carefully hid the treasure, and after abandoning the ark, he recovered it from the place where he had hidden it. *Cecco d'Ascoli*, in Chapter IV of his commentary on the sphere of *Sarabusco*, says that he had seen a book on *Magic* written by *Ham;* he taught this science to his son *Misrain*. It is also said that *Ham* was the first *alchemist*. In *Exodus*, Chapters VII and VIII, we read that during the ten plagues of *Egypt* the first three miracles of *Moses* were imitated by the Magicians.

The Wise Men From Babylon

Certain *Chaldean* wise men from *Babylon*, having been admitted to the practice of judicial *Astrology*, devoted themselves also to the study of *Magic, Occult sciences, Sorcery* and *Charms*. These famous wise men could avert misfortunes and secure all kinds of benefits by means of Magical ceremonies.

Isaiah, Chapter XLVII, foretold the destruction of *Babylon;* owing to the great number of its sorcerers and the multitude of its Magicians.

In the tenth song of *Homer's Odyssey* appears *Circe*, who changes men into animals; further on we find certain *Conjurations* for stopping, by means of mysterious songs, the bleeding of a wound.

Medea rejuvenated the body of *Eson*, according to

Euripides; she sent to *Glauca* (daughter of a *Corinthian king,* for whom Jason had repudiated her) a gown and a crown contaminated with an evil curse which caused her death. According to the demonographers she had learned Sorcery from her mother *Hecate*. In *Alceste* we find that in *Thessaly* there were psychogogues who by means of ablutions and *charms* caused shades to appear or drove them away.

Within historic times, *Democritus* was considered to be devoted to the practice of *Magic* and to have written on the subject; *Pliny* also mentions *Pythagoras, Empedocles* and *Plato*.

Plutarch (on the delays of divine justice) says that the *Lacedemonians* brought sorcerers from *Thessaly,* so famous for its Magicians.

Before *Demosthenes,* who relates that the *Athenians* killed *Theorides,* a *Magician* of *Lemnos,* the *Greek* writers fail to mention any punishment inflicted upon *Magicians*.

It was after the conquests of *Alexander* that the *Magician Osthranes* made the *Persian* science known to the *Greeks*. *Magic* then became popular. All the *Greek* cities had their *Sorcerers*. *Ephesus* was the center of all the foreign "Witch-Craft" and "Black Arts," which were brought from *Asia* and spread throughout *Greece*. At the same time it made its way into *Egypt*.

The same invasion took place in the *Roman* world. *Nigidins Figulus,* the friend of *Cicero,* was one of the most enthusiastic partisans of the old world *Magic*. *Horace,* in the eighth satire of the first book, speaks of the practices followed in *Canidia* in the *Magical* arts. *Tiberius* prohibited the *Magicians* from practicing their art, because he feared their power. *Nero* called several *Sorcerers* to his court, among others being *Tiradatus;* after killing his father, he took rufuge in *Magic* against the spirit of *Aggripinus*. *Juvenal,* in satire V, teaches us that *Magic* was sullied by human sacrifices. *Horace* says that they went so far as to work wonders by *Magic*.

Apuleus, impelled by an insatiable desire of knowledge, had himself initiated in all of the mysteries. He went to *Athens* and to *Rome;* having married a widow, her parents sued him, accusing him of having made use of *Magic* and *Talismans* in order to make himself loved.

Triumphal Christianity restrained to some extent the advance made by *Magic;* it anathematized and persecuted all those who gave themselves to its practices, after the struggle of *Saint Peter* and *Simon* the *Magician;* under *Constantine* we find all *Occult* practices prohibited. But the horror which was manifested for *Sorcery* at that time increased the belief in it. In the *Middle Ages* every mind which distinguished itself by deep studies or by new ideas incurred the reproach of *Magic*.

In the eleventh century *Pope Gregory* VII was accused of *Magic* at the Council of Bixen. *Roger Bacon*, the inventor of gunpowder, was accused of having made with the aid of *Magic*, a bronze head which replied to his questions. *Albert* the *Great* was thought to have devised an artificial man, called *Android*. In the sixteenth century, *Cornelius Agrippa* was thought to have the devil constantly with him in the form of a *black dog*. Finally, in the following century, *Urban Grandier* was burnt alive after having been convicted of a crime of *Magic*.

Therefore it follows that *Magic* has flourished at all periods; it has given rise to a large number of *Occult sciences;* above all "*Talismanic Magic*," which is now in great favor, everything being subject to *Talismans, Signet Rings*, with an *Occult Symbol* Engraved thereon; *Three Headed Snake Magic Rings;* set with Diamonds, and other precious stones; hundreds of which are now being worn by *Occult* students all over the world. On the following pages there will be found abundant information, but the very same is only for the one whose intellect is clear and clean of religious dogmas and the coarse teachings of western materialism. *He who keeps this book constantly with him, will attract a good Occult power and influence.*

Some years ago, during a trip which I made through *Egypt,* I spent several weeks in *Constantinople.* During the short time that I remained in that wonderful city of *Eastern Mysteries* a certain man died. He had the reputation of being a famous *Sorcerer.* He also enjoyed a great prestige among his fellow citizens, and he had many clients among the very rich and well to do element of the city who came to him for advice and help. Having been an old *Egyptian* priest, he had learned, in cities throughout the *Orient,* during the rare intervals of peace which occurred in that glorious epoch of our history, to practice *Talismanic Magic.* A shepherd before his departure, he returned as a dreaded *Sorcerer.* He devoted himself to this art, but I must admit that everyone, peasants as well as the city officials, believed in his wonderful *Occult* powers. He, the old *Egyptian,* was very close mouthed about his secrets, for he was very desirous of maintaining his prestige, and he could only do so by being careful in the use of his famous *Talismans and Seals.* Upon his death his few possessions, which included an *Ancient Manuscript* showing how he made his *Talismans* from *Virgin Parchment,* were sold. Anxious to enter "*The Cave of the Oracle,*" I attended the sale and was not a little surprised to hear announced, among the *Matthew Laensberg, Pierre Larrivay* and other *Ancient Manuscripts,* by the old Egyptian the one known as "THE CAVE OF THE ORACLE," dealing briefly but exclusively on the above subjects. I now understood where the Egyptian had acquired his knowledge

OCCULTISM AND MAGIC

and I hastened to purchase the musty *Manuscript* at a high price. I was especially glad to do so, I assure you, since it was rare, and of very great value. It is from this work that I am going to give you some secret instruction for making your own *Talismans and Seals*. I will commence with the *Talismans*, in the words of the old *Egyptian*, as follows: "No one dares to doubt that the *Stars* and *Planets* do exert a dominant influence upon everything on the earth; because, inasmuch as it is clearly evident that the *Planets* exert an *Occult* influence on men, women and children. These very same *Planets* also exert a most powerful unseen influence on all *Talismans, Charms and Seals* whenever they are reproduced on genuine Virgin Parchment Paper, made with the skin of a *dead-born* lamb and deeply imbued with the odor of burning *Oriental Temple Incense*."

People should know the great value of these things such as *Talismans and Seals* in order to draw the invisible influences of Nature into a *Talisman* or *Seal*. But what is most worthy of notice is that the *Planets* never exert their unseen influence so efficiently as when genuine Virgin Parchment Paper, made from the skin of a *dead-born* lamb, is used to construct the Talisman. The skin of a dead lamb is much in sympathy with the *Occult* or invisible forces of Nature and the wise *Kabalists* knowing this secret always used genuine *Virgin Parchment Paper* made from the skin of a *dead-born* lamb.

CHAPTER II

TALISMANS

THEIR POWER AND INFLUENCE

THE *"Telesma,"* or *Talisman,* was anciently held in great esteem by the Thaumaturgists. We find evidence of its universality in *China, India, Egypt,* and among the Semitic nations, the Greeks and Romans, as well as among the ancient populace of *Central America, Peru, Australasia,* and the islands of the Pacific. Indeed, there seems every reason to believe that *Talismanic Magic* was in vogue among the *Atlanteans,* and by them transmitted to the surviving nations. It comes to us in a modified form from the *Hebrews,* who adapted it to their own theological system. A brief account of the principles of this art and its methods can hardly be omitted from a work of this character, inasmuch as it is directly connected with *Astrology* and the construction of *Talismans,* and forms a very important part of the equipment of the *magus.*

Necessarily the mind of man must have concrete methods of expression; the most common and limited of which is language. *Symbolism,* on the other hand, may be regarded as the common language of humanity, as also it is that of the Spirits of the Astral Plane. The universe is a symbol; so also is man. *Color, Number,* and *Form*—what are they but *symbols? A circle, triangle, a square, a cross*—these are but letters in an universal language, the only natural medium by which we can compel the notice of the spirits. Such was the belief of the *Pythagoreans* and the *Thaumaturgists* of ancient *Greece*.

The *Kabala,* or secret interpretation, is divided into three sections: The *Gimetria,* the *Notaricon,* and the *Temurah.* It will be necessary to know these before entering upon *Talismanic Magic,* for nothing is brought to perfection in this art without the magical use of names and numbers.

By *Magical* use we are to understand something in distinction from natural use, as the difference between the supreme power of the creative will in man and the inherent vegetative power of the soul and of natural bodies.

First, then, let us examine the principles of the *Kabala.* Man is the subject of all magical considerations, as he is also the agent of all magical operations. The *Kabalists* divide Man into four principles—viz. *Spirit, Mind, Soul,* and *Body,* corresponding to the four "elements" of *Fire, Air, Water,* and *Earth.* Of these the *Spirit* and *Mind* are *Formless,* and the *Fluidic Body* or *Soul* and the Physical Body are *Formative.* Yet there are three aspects of the Spirit, viz. *Life, Will,* and *Effort,* and three aspects of the Mind, viz. *Perception, Reason,* and *Memory.* So also the properties of the *Soul* are three: *Desire, Imagination,* and *Emotion;* and of the Body three: *Absorption, Circulation,* and *Secretion.* For in one aspect Nature is *volatile,* in another *fixed,* and in another *mutable.*

Humanity consists of three orders: *Lapsed Souls, Elementary Souls,* and *Demoniacal Souls.* We distinguish between the Spirit and the Soul. The Spirit in itself is of *Divine* origin, a scintilla of some spiritual hierarchy to which it is directly related and from which it receives its energy and direction. These *"imprisoned lights"* are related to *Deity* through the spiritual hierarchies to which they severally belong and of which they are the earthly representatives.

The *Soul,* on the other hand, is not of Divine origin, but is derived mediately from the nature-essence through the operation of the Human Imagination, or —as in the case of the brute creation—by Desire and the instinctual sense.

Lapsed Souls are such as have fallen from their first estate or pristine nature, and will, by regeneration, eventually regain their lost heritage.

Elementary Souls are such as have come into human generation in the course of natural evolution or by *Magical Art,* and of these the *Sylphides* are such as neighbor the human race most nearly. Coming as strangers into an atmosphere for which their powers are not yet sufficiently evolved, they are born as naturals, simpletons and fools, a condition which is successively improved during their human incarnations. Once entangled in the human system of evolution, they cannot go back. By this humanity of theirs they acquire an immortality not otherwise attainable. Of the same category of *Elementaries* are the *Undines, Salamanders,* and *Gnomes,* these names being related to the elements of *Water, Fire* and *Earth,* as *Sylphs* to that of *Air.*

Demoniacal Souls are such as have by violence thrust themselves into human life by *obsessions,* overshadowings and infestings of the bodies of men, whether in *frenzy* or in *trance,* in *epilepsy* or other abnormal conditions of the mind and body. *They are like robbers who take possession of the house while the owner is away.* But some such are born into the world by the will of the gods, operating by means of sidereal influences, for the fulfilling of large destinies, the despoiling and punishing of nations, and are demons from their birth. Concerning such an one the *Christ* said: "*You twelve have I chosen, and one of you is a devil,*" meaning *Judas Iscariot.** From this it will be seen

---

*Judas Iscariot, the disciple who betrayed *Christ* for 30 pieces of silver. *Luke* XXII, 3.

that not all human forms are invested with human souls.

Also there are certain times and seasons when angels and archangels are temporarily invested with the human flesh for the high purposes of life, some as teachers and prophets, others as messengers of peace; but all such are free from the taint of the soul while obeying the laws of their mortal selfhood, yet acting in all else under the direct inspiration of the Spirit. Of such high order was *Melchizedek*, the King of Righteousness, *"without father and without mother, having neither beginning of life nor end of days,"* with whom *Abraham* talked as recorded in the *Genesis*. *Melchizedek* was, in fact, a presentation of the *Christ*, a great and mighty spirit in temporary human form then reigning in *Chaldea* over the sons and daughters of the *Magi*.

But also there are those spirits of the nature of *Apollyon*, who are *"Princes of Darkness,"* and whose dominion is over those *"wandering stars for whom is laid up the blackness of darkness for ages upon ages."* These malevolent beings, acting under the laws of their own nature, do from time to time manifest in human form for a more speedy judgment of the world. They are the *Caligulas* and *Neros* of the world's history.

The earth is therefore the theatre of a great variety of different souls, and is such because it is in equilibrium between the Heavens and the Hells, and in a state of freedom where good and evil may commingle. It is in truth the Field of Armageddon, where must be fought out the great battle between the Powers of Light and the Powers of Darkness.

The *Kabalists* mention Seven Heavens and Seven Hells, presided over by the Seven Archangels and the Seven Princes of Evil. The Archangels of the Seven Spheres of Light are: *Michael, Gabriel, Kamiel,*

Raphael, Zadkiel, Uriel, and *Zophkiel,* standing for the Might, Grace, Zeal, Saving Power, Justice, Splendor, and Mystery of Nature (God). These names are invoked under appropriate *symbols* in *Talismanic Magic* of which the *Kabala* forms an essential part.

Michael, the archangel associated with the *Sun,* is derived from the syllables *Mi,* who; *cah,* like; *al,* god; *i.e.* He who is like unto God; or Who is like unto him? Gabriel, from *Gibur,* power; Kamiel, from *Chem* or *Kam,* heat; Raphael, from *Raphah,* healing; Zadkiel, from *Zadok,* justice; Uriel, from *Aur,* light; and Zophkiel, from *Zophek,* a secret. As spiritual entities they are the express embodiments of the Divine attributes, though while unrevealed to us they continue only to stand for certain human conceptions of the Divine Being expressed in terms of human character. All definition is limitation, and all limitation is imperfection, yet God is the only Perfection and beyond all naming.

VIRGIN PARCHMENT

An ancient *Egyptian Kabalist,* or maker of *Talismans* and *Charms,* constructed their *Talismans* and *Charms* on genuine *Virgin Parchment,* made from the skin of new-born lambs, as follows: For making a *Talisman* under the influence of the *Sun* they chose *Sunday* for the day, and *Oriental Gold Ink* to trace the figure on genuine *Virgin Parchment* Paper. For making a *Talisman* under the influence of the *Moon* they chose Monday for the day, and *Seal Brown Ink* for tracing the *Talisman.* For making a *Talisman* under the influence of *Mars,* they chose Tuesday for the day, and *Violet Ink* to trace the figure on the *Talisman.* For making a *Talisman* under the influence of *Mercury,* they chose Wednesday for the day, and *Pale-blue*

Ink to trace the figure on the *Talisman*. For making a *Talisman* under the influence of *Jupiter*, they chose Thursday for the day, and *Oriental Red Ink* for tracing the *Talisman;* for *Oriental Red Ink* corresponds most nearly to copper in color. For making a *Talisman* under the influence of *Venus*, they chose Friday for the day, and *Brilliant Green Ink* to trace the figure on the *Talisman*. For making a *Talisman* under the influence of *Saturn*, they chose Saturday for the day, and *Magic Black Ink* to trace the figure on the *Talisman*. As stated above, nothing else was used or considered of value for the construction of these famous Talismans of the ancients, except genuine *Virgin Parchment Paper*, made from the skin of *dead-born* lambs, traced with the very colored ink set out and described herein. These very same *Talismans* were traced on squares of genuine *Parchment Paper* exactly 3x3 inches in size, and worn on the breast, under the clothing, suspended from the neck in a pure Hand-Made Silk Bag. As hereinafter shown, instruction will be given for the day of the week, the hour of the day or night in which a *Talisman* may be made, for every day in the week and the use to which it can be put to by the sincere student. It must be understood, however, that the student must have absolute faith in the working efficacy of the *Talisman* he constructs according to the instruction and direction set down herein for his benefit. *"Works without faith are useless."* So *Talismans* constructed according to the rules of the *Ancient Kabalists, without faith carry with them an influence that works against the one who wears them.*

As stated elsewhere, *Talismans* should be made upon genuine *Virgin Parchment Paper* and produced most accurately. *Talismans*, as well as precious stones, may be employed for *Amulets;* but the *Talisman* must be kept in a *Silken Bag* of a *Purple* color and preserved from all impure glances and contacts. Thus, *Talismans* and *Pentacles* after having been produced on *Virgin Parchment Paper* must not be seen or touched by deformed or misshapen persons, or by immoral women. *Talismans* may be profaned by the looks and hands of debauched men and menstruating females. They will also lose their virtue if seen or touched by an enemy and they must be concealed from cowards and disbelievers. *Talismans* should not be touched by the hands of depraved men and men under a vow of celibacy. It is well to keep all *Talismans* away from the impious, neither should they be touched by a person who is not fully in sympathy with you in everything that you do. The large number of ancient *Talismans* being worn now by my *Chela's* (Disciples) of true "*Occultism*" is worthy of comment. "*Blessed are they who believe,*" said the great Master of *Nazareth*. They, who today, believe in *Talismans*, and have strong faith in them will be *doubly blessed;* for *Talismans* are like crosses of honor and other kindred decorations which increase the wearer's personal value and merit. The *Talisman* which has been properly and accurately constructed is of great value, for Nature imparts to the *Talisman* a prodigious power and influence. Sufficient attention has not been paid to the reciprocal influence of *Talismans*, for they are the symbol of *Occult* sovereignty. *Talismans* are a most important *Magical* instrument when constructed according to the operations of *Transcendent* and divine *Magic*.

* * * * * * * * * *

On the front side of each of the seven *Talismans*, one for each day of the week, as herein described, there must be traced, with the particular *Ink* suited to the *Planet*, a square which contains the mysterious number of the *Planet* under which it is made. These are plainly given under each day of the week, and the

Talisman is to be printed on a square of genuine *Virgin Parchment Paper*, 3x3 inches in size. On the reverse, or opposite side, you are to inscribe the *Planetary Seal*, and *Sigil* of the *Planetary* intelligence. By studying the directions given under each day of the week, you will have no trouble in understanding how the *Talismans*, hereinafter referred to, are to be made. You are admonished however, to make them exactly as directed, and in no other-wise. Again, the *Talisman* after being constructed, should be fumigated with the fumes of burning *Oriental Temple Incense*. This is accomplished by putting one-half teaspoonful of Incense in the burner, lighting it, and holding the *Talisman* about eighteen inches above the burner, but directly in the fumes and smoke of the burning *Incense*. The *Talisman* should be held in this position for about five minutes. It should then be enclosed in a special case made from prepared *Tympan Paper*. *Tympan Paper* protects the *Talisman* from bodily perspiration, moisture and undue dampness, so that it will not be affected by atmospheric changes. The *Talisman* thus constructed, should then be enclosed in a *Pure Silk Hand Made Bag,* and worn on the breast, suspended from the neck, until such time as its operation is effected, when it is to be regarded as a *"dead" Talisman,* and thereafter will serve for no other person or purpose. Now, let it be understood that full directions for making these *Talismans* are given on the following pages. Further, the description and price of the materials needed such as, squares of genuine *Virgin Parchment Paper, Oriental Temple Incense,* the different colored *inks*, specially prepared *Tympan Paper,* and *Pure Silk Hand Made Bags,* are fully set forth on a certain page in the back of this book, to which the student is referred. All the materials herein before referred to, are of the highest quality and are guaranteed to be absolutely genuine.

TALISMAN FOR SUNDAY

THE SEAL OF THE SUN

This *Talisman* must be constructed exactly as directed below, no other material being used than that named herein; neither are you to use anything otherwise than *Oriental Temple Incense* for to fumigate and imbue the same. This *Talisman* must be thoroughly tinged and saturated with the suffumes of burning *Temple Incense,* and worn on the breast underneath the clothing, suspended from the neck in a *Pure Silk Hand Made Bag.*

6	32	3	34	45	1
7	11	27	28	8	30
19	14	16	15	23	24
18	20	22	21	17	13
25	29	10	9	26	2
36	5	23	4	2	31

Front Side Of Talisman For Sunday.

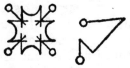

Seal Of The Sun.
Back Side Of Talisman For Sunday.

First, take a square piece of pure *Virgin Parchment Paper,* 3x3 inches in size, which must be clean and unspotted on both sides. On the front you are to trace with *Oriental Gold Ink* a square, such as is shown here, comprising six lines of figures, so that by counting the figures from one corner to the other, in the form of *St. Andrews'* cross, the sum found will be one hundred and eleven. The mysterious part of this, and of which the student should be informed, is that the numbers which are marked in all *Talismans* and *Seals* of the *Planets,* are the numbers of the great *Stars* which are under the domination of each *Planet,* and which Nature assigns to them as their subjects; and it is for this reason that persons versed in *Egyptian and Hindu Astrology* call the *Planets* heralds of first *Stars*. For they have the others under their control for the free distribution of their influence. Now, as stated above, let the student proceed to trace the squares and numbers shown herein on the front side of a piece of *Virgin Parchment*. On the back side of the square piece of *Parchment* you are to trace with *Oriental Gold Ink,* the *Seal Of The Sun* exactly as shown herein. In order that this operation may be executed exactly according to the rules of the *Cabala* and under the proper conditions, you must have in your possession, some *Temple Incense* and a burner of good ventilation, so as to make a suitable fumigation for the *Talisman,* after it has been constructed according to the rules laid down herein, and, in accordance with everything that I have said above. In order not to lose the favorable time this *Talisman* must be traced on genuine *Parchment Paper,* and fumigated with *Temple Incense* during the first hour of *Sunday* morning. That is, between the hours of 12 and 1 A. M. *Sunday*. The very same should be made at the hour stated above on the first Sunday of any month of the twelve months in a year. That is to say, that you are only to make this *Talisman* on the first hour of the morning of the first *Sunday* of any month. It must be borne in mind that it is at this hour that the *Planet* sends forth its benign influence on the *Talisman* in a positive and mysterious manner, providing the same is properly imbued with the exquisite odor of *Burning Temple Incense*. The properties of this *Talisman*, of the *Sun,* consists in the fact that the person who wears it with faith and reverence, will become agreeable to the powerful people and great ones around them, whose good will he wishes to secure. Let this *Talisman* be constructed in strict accordance with the rules laid down and set forth herein, and worn in a *Pure Silk Hand Made Bag,* secretly under thy clothing, as stated above, and you will, so it is said by the *Ancients,* acquire wealth and honor and will be respected by all with whom you come in contact, *providing you perform these sacred acts with faith and great reverence.*

To obtain the favorable results, the *Talisman* described herein, should without fail, first be traced with *Oriental Gold Ink,* which is a color analogous to that of the spirit of the *Sun,* and then enclosed in a case made from special prepared *Tympan Paper,* to protect the *Talisman* from undue dampness, caused by the perspiration or sweat from the body, as well as from moisture. A *Talisman* enclosed in this *Tympan Paper* is not affected by atmospheric conditions, as it resists dampness. After enclosing the *Talisman* in *Tympan Paper,* the same can then be placed in a *Pure Silk Hand Made Bag,* and be worn secretly under thy clothing, suspended from thy neck.

TYMPAN PAPER. This paper has been obtained by Dr. de Laurence, to protect *Talismans* against bodily perspiration, sweat and dampness, as it is not affected by the atmospheric conditions, and resists moisture. The *Talisman* then remains *clean and unspotted,* as well as unaffected by anything whatsoever, as *Tympan Paper* is both moisture and water-proof. This paper is very expensive, and is only furnished upon request. Those who wish it, as well as squares of genuine *Virgin Parchment Paper,* and a *Pure Silk Hand Made Bag,* will find particulars regarding these things, and also genuine *Temple Incense,* and various colored *Inks,* upon a certain page in the back of this book.

TALISMANS 31

TALISMAN FOR MONDAY

THE SEAL OF THE MOON

This *Talisman* must be constructed exactly as directed below, no other material being used than that named herein; neither are you to use anything otherwise than *Oriental Temple Incense* for to fumigate and imbue the same. This Talisman must be thoroughly tinged and saturated with the suffumes of burning *Temple Incense*, and worn on the breast underneath the clothing, suspended from the neck in a *Pure Silk Hand Made Bag*.

First, take a square piece of pure *Virgin Parchment Paper*, 3x3 inches in size, which must be clean and unspotted on both sides. On the front side you are to trace with *Seal Brown Ink* a square, such as is

27	78	26	70	21	62	12	54	5
6	38	28	30	71	22	63	14	46
47	7	39	80	31	72	23	55	15
16	48	8	40	8	32	64	24	56
57	17	49	9	41	73	33	65	25
26	53	18	50	1	42	74	34	66
67	27	59	10	51	2	43	75	35
36	68	19	60	11	52	3	44	76
77	28	69	60	61	12	53	4	45

Front Side Of Talisman For Monday.

Seal Of The Moon.
Back Side Of Talisman For Monday.

shown here, so that it will contain the mysterious number, of the *Moon* which is three hundred and sixty-nine, as represented herewith. It will be noticed that this mysterious square has nine certain numbers each way, and that they are written in the eighty-one squares. In the construction of this *Talisman* you are to write or trace this on your square of *Parchment* exactly as it is printed herewith. On the back of the piece of *Virgin Parchment Paper* you are to trace, with Seal Brown Ink, the *Seal Of The Moon* exactly as shown herein. In order that this operation may be executed exactly according to the rules of the *Cabala* and under the proper conditions, you must have in your possession, some *Temple Incense* and a burner of good ventilation, so as to make a suitable fumigation for the *Talisman* after it has been constructed according to the rules laid down herein, and, in accordance with everything that I have said above. In order not to lose the favorable time, this *Talisman* must be traced on genuine *Parchment Paper*, and fumigated with *Temple Incense* during the first hour of *Monday* morning. That is, between the hours of 12 and 1 A. M. *Monday*. The very same should be made at the hour stated above on the first *Monday* of any month of the twelve months in a year. That is to say, that you are only to make this *Talisman* on the first Monday of any month. It must be borne in mind that it is at this hour that the *Planet* sends forth its benign influence on the *Talisman* in a positive and mysterious manner, providing the same is properly imbued with the exquisite odor of *Burning Temple Incense*. The properties of this particular *Talisman*, of the *Moon*, consists in the fact that the one who wears it with faith and reverence, will find it very useful to preserve them against the common diseases. That is, if worn with absolute and literal faith in its efficacy, it assists the wearer in becoming immune to certain abnormal pathological conditions. As the author of this work is a well-learned pathologist, this *Talisman*, no doubt, will serve the purpose for which it was created. It is also used to guard travelers against dangers and attacks of thieves, and will be most useful to farmers and merchants.

To obtain the most favorable results, the *Talisman* described herein, should, without fail, first be traced with *Seal Brown Ink*, which is a color analogous to that of the spirit of the *Moon*, and then enclosed in a case made from special prepared *Tympan Paper*, to protect the *Talisman* from undue dampness, caused by the perspiration or sweat from the body, as well as from moisture. A *Talisman* enclosed in this *Tympan Paper* is not affected by atmospheric conditions, as it resists dampness. After enclosing the *Talisman* in *Tympan Paper*, the same can then be placed in a *Pure Silk Hand Made Bag*, and be worn secretly under thy clothing, suspended from thy neck.

TYMPAN PAPER. This paper has been obtained by DR. DE LAURENCE, to protect *Talismans* against bodily perspiration, sweat and dampness, as it is not affected by the atmospheric conditions, and resists moisture. The *Talisman* then remains *clean and unspotted*, as well as unaffected by anything whatsoever, as *Tympan Paper* is both moisture and water-proof. This paper is very expensive, and is only furnished upon request. Those who wish it, as well as squares of genuine *Virgin Parchment Paper*, and a *Pure Silk Hand Made Bag*, will find particulars regarding these things, and also genuine *Temple Incense*, and various colored *Inks*, upon a certain page in the back of this book.

34 THE CAVE OF THE ORACLE

TALISMAN FOR TUESDAY

THE SEAL OF MARS

This *Talisman* must be constructed exactly as directed below, no other material being used than that named herein; neither are you to use anything otherwise than *Oriental Temple Incense* for to fumigate and imbue the same. This *Talisman* must be thoroughly tinged and saturated with the suffumes of burning *Temple Incense,* and worn on the breast underneath the clothing, suspended from the neck in a *Pure Silk Hand Made Bag.*

14	10	1	22	18
20	11	7	3	24
21	17	13	9	5
2	23	19	15	6
8	4	25	16	12

Front Side Of Talisman For Tuesday.

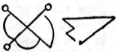

Seal Of Mars.
Back Side Of Talisman For Tuesday.

First, take a square piece of pure *Virgin Parchment Paper,* 3x3 inches in size, which must be clean and unspotted on both sides. On the front side you are to trace with *Violet Ink* a square, such as is shown here, so that it will contain the mysterious number of the *Planet Mars* which is sixty-five, as shown herewith. It will be noticed that this mysterious square has five certain numbers each way, and that they are written in the twenty-five squares. In the construction of this *Talisman* you are to write or trace this *Talisman* on your square of *Parchment* exactly as it is printed herewith. On the back side of the piece of *Virgin Parchment Paper* you are to trace, with *Violet Ink,* the *Seal Of Mars* exactly as shown herein. In order that this operation may be executed exactly according to the rules of the *Cabala* and under the proper conditions, you must have in your possession, some *Temple Incense* and a burner of good ventilation, so as to make a suitable fumigation for the *Talisman* after it has been constructed according to the rules laid down herein, and, in accordance with everything that I have said above. In order not to lose the favorable time, this *Talisman* must be traced on genuine *Virgin Parchment Paper,* and fumigated with *Temple Incense* during the first hour of Tuesday morning. That is, between the hours of 12 and 1 A. M. *Tuesday.* The very same should be made at the hour stated above on the first *Tuesday* of any month of the twelve months in a year. That is to say, that you are only to make this *Talisman* on the first *Tuesday* of any month.

It must be borne in mind that it is at this hour that the *Planet* sends forth its benign influence on the *Talisman* in a positive and mysterious manner, providing the same is properly imbued with the exquisite odor of *Burning Temple Incense.* The properties of this particular *Talisman,* of *Mars,* consists in the fact that the one who wears it with faith and reverence, will be rendered invulnerable, giving him extraordinary strength and vigor, and he will be victorious in all his combats. The influence of *Mars* upon this *Talisman* is so wonderful, when worn suspended from the neck the one who wears it thus will be impregnable, and those who try to overcome him will be easily routed. If this very same *Talisman* is made between the hours of four and five on *Tuesday* morning, that is, the very first Tuesday in any month, it then is in opposition with favorable and contrary *Planets,* it carries evil wherever it is taken, and it causes dissensions, revolts and separation wherever it is placed.

To obtain the most favorable results, the *Talisman* described herein, should, without fail, first be traced in *Violet Ink,* which is a color analogous to that of the Planet Mars, and then enclosed in a case made from special prepared *Tympan Paper,* to protect the *Talisman* from undue dampness, caused by the perspiration or sweat from the body, as well as from moisture. A *Talisman* enclosed in this *Tympan Paper* is not affected by atmospheric conditions, as it resists dampness. After enclosing the *Talisman* in *Tympan Paper,* the same can then be placed in a *Pure Silk Hand Made Bag,* and be worn secretly under thy clothing, suspended from thy neck.

TYMPAN PAPER. This paper has been obtained by DR. DE LAURENCE, to protect *Talismans* against bodily perspiration, sweat and dampness, as it is not affected by the atmospheric conditions, and resists moisture. The *Talisman* then remains clean and unspotted, as well as unaffected by anything whatsoever, as *Tympan Paper* is both moisture and water-proof. This paper is very expensive, and is only furnished upon request. Those who wish it, as well as squares of genuine *Virgin Parchment Paper,* and a *Pure Silk Hand Made Bag,* will find particulars regarding these things, and also genuine *Temple Incense,* and various colored Inks, upon a certain page in the back of this book.

TALISMAN FOR WEDNESDAY

THE SEAL OF MERCURY

This *Talisman* must be constructed exactly as directed below, no other material being used than that named herein; neither are you to use anything otherwise than *Oriental Temple Incense* for to fumigate and imbue the same. This *Talisman* must be thoroughly tinged and saturated with the suffumes of burning *Temple Incense*, and worn on the breast underneath the clothing, suspended from the neck in a *Pure Silk Hand Made Bag*.

8	58	59	5	4	62	63	1
49	15	14	52	53	11	10	56
41	23	22	44	45	19	18	48
32	34	35	29	28	38	39	25
40	26	27	37	36	30	31	33
57	47	46	20	21	33	42	24
9	54	54	12	13	51	50	16
64	2	3	61	60	6	7	57

Front Side of Talisman for Wednesday.

Seal of Mercury.
Back Side of Talisman for Wednesday.

First, take a square piece of pure *Virgin Parchment Paper,* 3x3 inches in size, which must be clean and unspotted on both sides. On the front side you are to trace with *Pale-Blue Ink* a square, such as is shown here, so that it will contain the mysterious number of *Mercury* which is two hundred and sixty and is distributed throughout sixty-four squares as shown herewith. It will be noticed that this mysterious square has eight certain numbers each way, and that they are written in the sixty-four squares. In the construction of this *Talisman* you are to write or trace it on your square of *Parchment* exactly as it is printed herewith. On the back side of the piece of *Virgin Parchment Paper* you are to trace, with *Pale-Blue Ink*, the *Seal of Mercury* exactly as shown herein. In order that this operation may be executed exactly according to the rules of the *Cabala* and under the proper conditions, you must have in your possession, some *Temple Incense* and a burner of good ventilation, so as to make a suitable fumigation for the *Talisman* after it has been constructed according to the rules laid down herein, and in accordance with everything that I have said above. In order not to lose the favorable time, this *Talisman* must be traced on genuine *Parchment Paper*, and fumigated with *Temple Incense* during the first hour of *Wednesday* morning. That is, between the hours of 12 and 1 A. M. *Wednesday*. The very same should be made at the hour stated above on the first *Wednesday* of any month of the twelve months in a year. That is to say, that you are only to make this *Talisman* on the first *Wednesday* of any month. It must be borne in mind that it is at this hour that the Planet sends forth its benign influence on the *Talisman* in a positive and mysterious manner, providing the same is properly imbued with the exquisite odor of *Burning Temple Incense*. The properties of this particular *Talisman*, of *Mercury* will render the reverent and faithful bearer thereof discreet and eloquent, and will prepare them admirably to become learned in all manner of sciences, and those things taught in all books of learning. If this *Talisman* is constructed exactly as laid down herein, and fumigated with *Oriental Temple Incense,* as set forth herein, it is said to cause the memory to become better, so that the retentive powers of memory will retain with ease what one wishes, especially if the same is placed under the pillow at night while the owner thereof is asleep. Furthermore, it is recommended to those who wish to be instructed by the spirits while asleep, so that certain information and other things one wishes to know will be given to them in a dream. No doubt this is a very valuable *Talisman* and as it can be quite easily constructed at a small cost, there will be many who will avail themselves of the opportunity to possess one forthwith. These things are not for the foolish and must not be treated as mere trifles, and those who take this view, should save themselves from trouble, otherwise their efforts will avail them nothing.

To obtain the favorable results, the *Talisman* described herein, should, without fail, first be traced in *Pale-Blue Ink,* which is a color analogous to that of the spirit of *Mercury,* and then enclosed in a case made from special prepared *Tympan Paper,* to protect the Talisman from undue dampness, caused by the perspiration or sweat from the body, as well as from moisture. A *Talisman* enclosed in this *Tympan Paper* is not affected by atmospheric conditions, as it resists dampness. After enclosing the *Talisman* in *Tympan Paper,* the same can then be placed in a *Pure Silk Hand Made Bag,* and be worn secretly under thy clothing, suspended from thy neck.

TYMPAN PAPER. This paper has been obtained by Dr. de Laurence, to protect *Talismans* against bodily perspiration, sweat and dampness, as it is not affected by the atmospheric conditions, and resists moisture. The *Talisman* then remains clean and unspotted, as well as unaffected by anything whatsoever, as *Tympan Paper* is both moisture and water-proof.

TALISMAN FOR THURSDAY

THE SEAL OF JUPITER

This *Talisman* must be constructed exactly as directed below, no other material being used than that named herein; neither are you to use anything otherwise than *Oriental Temple Incense* for to fumigate and imbue the same. This *Talisman* must be thoroughly tinged and saturated with the suffumes of burning *Temple Incense,* and worn on the breast underneath the clothing suspended from the neck in a *Pure Silk Hand Made Bag.*

16	3	2	3
5	10	11	8
9	6	7	12
4	15	14	1

Front Side of Talisman for Thursday.

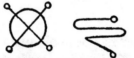

Seal of Jupiter. Back Side of Talisman for Thursday.

First, take a square piece of pure *Virgin Parchment Paper,* 3x3 inches in size, which must be clean and unspotted on both sides. On the front side you are to trace with *Oriental Red Ink* a square, such as is shown here, so that it will contain the mysterious number of the *Planet Jupiter,* which is thirty-four, distributed throughout sixteen squares as shown herewith. It will be noticed that this mysterious square has four certain numbers each way, and that they are written in the sixteen squares. In the construction of this *Talisman* you are to write or trace these squares on your square of *Parchment* exactly as they are printed herewith. On the back side of the piece of *Virgin Parchment Paper,* you are to trace, with *Oriental Red Ink,* the *Seal Of Jupiter* exactly as shown herein. In order that this operation may be executed exactly according to the rules of the Cabala and under the proper conditions, you must have in your possession, some *Temple Incense* and a burner of good ventilation, so as to make a suitable fumigation for the *Talisman* after it has been constructed according to the rules laid down herein, and, in accordance with everything that I have said above. In order not to lose the favorable time, this Talisman must be traced on genuine *Parchment Paper,* and fumigated with *Temple Incense* during the first hour of *Thursday* morning. That is, between the hours of 12 and 1 A. M. *Thursday.* The very same should be made at the hour stated above on the first *Thursday* of any month of the twelve months in a year. That is to say, that you are only to make this *Talisman* on the first *Thursday* of any month. It must be borne in mind that it is at this hour that the Planet sends forth its benign influence on the *Talisman* in a positive and mysterious manner, providing the same is properly imbued with the exquisite odor of *Burning Temple Incense.* The properties of this particular *Talisman, of Jupiter* will secure for those who construct it with faith and carry it reverently, the love and good will of those from whom it is desired. This *Talisman* is said to have the power, if thoroughly imbued with the suffumes of *Burning Oriental Temple Incense,* of multiplying one's possessions, such as money and other things as well as increasing one's spiritual and physical powers. This being true, it will bring success in business, commerce, and all other enterprises; it was used by the ancients to dissipate sorrow, harassing worries, and fear.

To obtain the favorable results, the *Talisman* described herein, should, without fail, first be traced in *Oriental Red Ink,* which is a color analogous to that of the spirit of the *Planet Jupiter,* and then enclosed in a case made from a special prepared *Tympan Paper,* to protect the *Talisman* from undue dampness, caused by the perspiration or sweat from the body, as well as from moisture. A *Talisman* enclosed in this *Tympan Paper* is not affected by atmospheric conditions, as it resists dampness. After enclosing the *Talisman* in *Tympan Paper,* the same can then be placed in a *Pure Silk Hand Made Bag,* and be worn secretly under thy clothing, suspended from thy neck.

TYMPAN PAPER. This paper has been obtained by Dr. de Laurence, to protect *Talismans* against bodily perspiration, sweat and dampness, as it is not affected by the atmospheric conditions, and resists moisture. The *Talisman* then remains clean and unspotted, as well as unaffected by anything whatsoever, as *Tympan Paper* is both moisture and waterproof. This paper is very expensive, and is only furnished upon request. Those who wish it, as well as squares of genuine *Virgin Parchment Paper,* and a *Pure Silk Hand Made Bag,* will find particulars regarding these things, and also genuine *Temple Incense,* and various colored *Inks,* upon a certain page in the back of this book.

TALISMANS

TALISMAN FOR FRIDAY

THE SEAL OF VENUS

This *Talisman* must be constructed exactly as directed below, no other material being used than that named herein; neither are you to use anything otherwise than *Oriental Temple Incense* for to fumigate and imbue the same. This *Talisman* must be thoroughly tinged and saturated with the suffumes of burning *Temple Incense,* and worn on the breast underneath the clothing, suspended from the neck in a *Pure Silk Hand Made Bag.*

First, take a square piece of pure *Virgin Parchment Paper,* 3x3 inches in size, which must be clean and unspotted on both sides. On the front side you are to trace with *Brilliant Green Ink* a square, such as is shown here, so that it will contain the mysterious number of the *Planet Venus,* which is

22	47	16	41	10	35	4
5	23	48	17	42	11	29
30	6	24	49	18	36	12
13	31	7	25	43	19	37
38	14	32	1	26	44	20
21	39	8	33	2	27	45
46	15	40	9	34	3	28

Front Side of Talisman for Friday.

Seal of Venus.
Back Side of Talisman for Friday.

seventy-five, distributed throughout forty-nine squares as shown herewith. It will be noticed that this mysterious square has seven certain numbers each way, and that they are written in the forty-nine squares. In the construction of this *Talisman* you are to write or trace these figures on your square of *Parchment* exactly as they are printed herewith. On the back side of the piece of *Virgin Parchment Paper*, you are to trace, with Brilliant Green Ink, the *Seal of Venus* exactly as shown herein.

In order that this operation may be executed exactly according to the rules of the *Cabala* and under the proper conditions, you must have in your possession, some *Temple Incense* and a burner of good ventilation, so as to make a suitable fumigation for the *Talisman* after it has been constructed according to the rules laid down herein, and in accordance with everything that I have said above. In order not to lose the favorable time, this *Talisman* must be traced on genuine *Parchment Paper*, and fumigated with *Temple Incense* during the first hour of *Friday* morning. That is, between the hours of 12 and 1 A. M. *Friday*. The very same should be made at the hour stated above on the first *Friday* of any month of the twelve months in a year. That is to say, that you are only to make this *Talisman* on the first *Friday* of any month. It must be borne in mind that it is at this hour that the *Planet* sends forth its benign influence on the *Talisman* in a positive and mysterious manner, providing the same is properly imbued with the exquisite odor of *Burning Temple Incense*. The properties of this particular *Talisman*, of *Venus*, will, without doubt, be greatly valued, and one who carries the very same with reverence and profound faith, may feel assured that they will win the good will from everyone from whom they desire it, and that they will be ardently loved, both by men and by women. It can also be used to reconcile mortal enmities, so that two persons become intimate friends; it also gives diligence and great ability in spiritual and astral powers, if constructed and worn as set forthwith herein.

To obtain the favorable results, the *Talisman* de-

TALISMANS

scribed herein, should, without fail, first be traced in *Brilliant Green Ink,* which is a color analogous to that of the spirit of the *Planet Venus,* and then enclosed in a case made from a special prepared *Tympan Paper,* to protect the *Talisman* from undue dampness, caused by the perspiration or sweat from the body, as well as from moisture. A *Talisman* enclosed in the *Tympan Paper* is not affected by atmospheric conditions, as it resists dampness. After enclosing the *Talisman* in *Tympan Paper,* the same can then be placed in a *Pure Silk Hand Made Bag,* and be worn secretly under thy clothing, suspended from thy neck.

TYMPAN PAPER. This paper has been obtained by Dr. de Laurence, to protect *Talismans* against bodily perspiration, sweat and dampness, as it is not affected by the atmospheric conditions, and resists moisture. The Talisman then remains clean and unspotted, as well as unaffected by anything whatsoever, as *Tympan Paper* is both moisture and water-proof. This paper is very expensive, and is only furnished upon request. Those who wish it, as well as squares of genuine *Virgin Parchment Paper,* and a *Pure Silk Hand Made Bag,* will find particulars regarding these things, and also genuine *Temple Incense,* and various *colored Inks,* upon a certain page in the back of this book.

TALISMAN FOR SATURDAY

THE SEAL OF SATURN

This *Talisman* must be constructed exactly as directed below, no other material being used than that named herein; neither are you to use anything otherwise than *Oriental Temple Incense* for to fumigate and imbue the same. This *Talisman* must be thoroughly tinged and saturated with the suffumes of burning *Temple Incense*, and worn on the breast underneath the clothing, suspended from the neck in a *Pure Silk Hand Made Bag*.

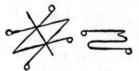

Front Side of Talisman for Saturday.

Seal of Saturn.
Back Side of Talisman for Saturday.

First, take a square piece of pure *Virgin Parchment Paper*, 3x3 inches in size, which must be clean and unspotted on both sides. On the front side you are to trace with *Magic Black Ink* a square, such as is shown here, so that it will contain the mysterious number of the *Planet Saturn*, which is fifteen, distributed throughout nine squares as shown herewith. It will be noticed that this mysterious square has three certain numbers each way, and that they are written in the nine squares. In the construction of this *Talisman* you are to write or trace these squares on your square of *Parchment* exactly as they are printed herewith. On the back side, of the piece of *Virgin Parchment Paper*, you are to trace, with *Magic Black Ink*, the *Seal Of Saturn*, exactly as shown herein.

In order not to lose the favorable time, this *Talis-*

man must be traced on genuine *Parchment Paper,* and fumigated with *Temple Incense* during the first hour of *Saturday* morning. That is, between the hours of 12 and 1 A. M. *Saturday*. The very same should be made at the hour stated above on the first *Saturday* of any month of the twelve months in a year. That is to say, that you are only to make this *Talisman* on the first Saturday of any month. It must be borne in mind that it is at this hour that the *Planet* sends forth its benign influence on the *Talisman* in a positive and mysterious manner, providing the same is properly imbued with the exquisite odor of *Burning Temple Incense*. The properties of this particular *Talisman,* of *Saturn,* are of great assistance to women suffering from the pains of childbirth, because with its aid, they find their pain very much lessened. This has been proved, so it is claimed, a number of times with great success by persons of high social standing who were subject to great pain, at this particular time. It is said to greatly help one to succeed in all affairs of life and that it multiplies and increases the things which one already is possessed of.

To obtain the favorable results, the *Talisman* described herein, should, without fail, first be traced in *Magic Black Ink,* which is a color analogous to that of the spirit of the *Planet Saturn,* and then enclosed in a case made from special prepared *Tympan Paper,* to protect the *Talisman* from undue dampness, caused by the perspiration or sweat from the body, as well as from moisture. A *Talisman* enclosed in this *Tympan Paper* is not affected by atmospheric conditions, as it resists dampness. After enclosing the *Talisman* in *Tympan Paper,* the same can then be placed in a *Pure Silk Hand Made Bag,* and be worn secretly under thy clothing, suspended from thy neck.

TYMPAN PAPER. This paper has been obtained by Dr. de Laurence, to protect *Talismans* against bodily perspiration, sweat and dampness, as it is not affected by the atmospheric conditions, and resists moisture. The *Talisman* then remains clean and unspotted, as well as unaffected by anything whatsoever, as *Tympan Paper* is both moisture and water-proof. This paper is very expensive, and is only furnished upon request. Those who wish it, as well as squares of genuine *Virgin Parchment Paper,* and a *Pure Silk Hand Made Bag,* will find particulars regarding these things, and also genuine *Temple Incense,* and various colored *Inks,* upon a certain page in the back of this book.

* * * * * * * * * * *

There are a number of things which have always offered great difficulty to the student who wished to make his own *Charms* and *Talismans,* such as securing the purest genuine *Virgin Parchment Paper,* made from the skin of *dead-born* lambs, as well as the suitable ink for tracing the *Talismans,* as well as the very figure which must be traced at a certain and given hour of the day or night. Of course, some difficulties must be expected in any undertaking, so it is with making *Talismans,* but when great results are to be obtained, the one who hesitates to overcome them, is necessarily of a very weak and cringing nature. Those who possess a weak personality never succeed well in life, but those whose nature is decisive and to the point, are the ones who carry out any instruction or advice given them, especially when it promotes their own welfare. The other kind of a person is a criminal, that is, they are guilty of a crime against their own self; for the greatest crime is indecision to carry out those things which promote both your own welfare and those who are around you, or dependent upon you. Of course the individual who dares to think for himself instead of allowing ministers and priests to think for him, recognizes the existence of an unseen but natural force which can be applied for the good or evil. *Evil powers caused by the astral congestions have invariably an anarchic and immoral tendency, because disorder invokes disorder, and evil invokes evil; so according to this immutable law, good invokes good.* Unless it is necessary to protect yourself against an enemy or an unscrupulous individual, you should never make use of a *Talisman* to produce bad effects.

Those who wish genuine *Virgin Parchment Paper*, cut into squares of the right dimensions to construct the *Talismans* shown herein, as well as colored ink, *Incense, burner, Tympan Paper,* and *Pure Silk Hand Made Bags*, will find these very same things listed together with the price and directions for ordering on a certain page in the back of this book.

Let the one who would construct a *Talisman*, first study carefully the directions set forth herein, then let them proceed with care and great deliberation, for nothing must be done hastily, neither shall it be performed without absolute faith and great interest. The *Ancients* taught that: *"He that hesitates is lost,"* as the scriptures tell of *Lot's* wife, who turned into a pillar of salt. *He who hesitates, and whose will is not firm, but faltering, invites and attracts demoralizing and destructive influences; for if you are not strong enough to overcome them, and are low in faith, they most certainly will overcome you.* Here is the great secret of wearing a *Talisman* and the old *Ancients* knew that their *Talismans*, when properly constructed, *did possess great virtue and that they served to arouse and stimulate the faith of the wearer.* Talismans are historical mediums of both good and evil, and the tradition and legend of *Seals* and *Amulets* bear out these statements.

The things spoken of herewith, are only for those whose soul is big, and good enough to believe in them-

selves and the unseen forces of Nature. For God is Nature and Nature is God.

To him who hath faith in the power within his own soul shall be given, and much will be added unto him, but he that hath not faith, even that which he hath, shall be taken from him. "Faith" itself begets the spiritual substance of things wanted. Fear and doubt attract those cold unrelentless forces which freeze the soul of the one who harbors it. The church man nowadays says that he believes in God, but a man need not be a church man to be a wise man, for many church men are far from being wise men. *A wise man believes neither in the church nor in God, but believes firmly in the power which lies within his own soul, for this, and only this, is God.* Jesus, the Jewish devotee, the greatest soul that ever lived and taught, and died, in the existing truth of humanity uttered the one cardinal principle which should attract all men. He said: *"Seek ye the Kingdom of God within ye."* The most scathing denunciation in the bible from *Genesis* to the last chapter of *Revelations* is: *"Ye of little faith." Christ, the Master, by faith, withered the fig tree.* A word to the wise is sufficient, and let all men whose eye reads this learn a lesson, and let them from now on to the end of their natural life, become a sincere investigator, and seek the *Kingdom* and power of *God*, not in the old superstitious teachings of the Jews of antiquity, *but in the depths of their own soul.*

THE MAIN POINTS IN MAGIC.

By whatever means we may constrain spiritual forces to our purpose, whether by *Sigil, Charm, Talisman* or *Invocation*, it is only by the faith of the operator, aided by the trained will and imagination, which are the *Magical* faculties of the human soul.

Imagination is the creative or formative power of the mind by which a matrix or mould is delivered to

TALISMANS

Nature for the vitalizing power of the *Will*. For of these faculties the imagination is female and receptive, while the will is masculine and projective. What in the common mind operates as desultory thought and desire, the thought taking form and the desire giving life to it, is replaced in the mind of the magician by an ardent will and conscious imagination directed to the creation of definite things. To a certain extent, all lovers, all poets and artists are magicians equally with the makers of empires and the reformers of the religious world. They have definite objects in view; their imaginations are fired with the vision of a thing greatly desired of them, and their wills are potent and effectually directed to the goal of their ambitions. These are the people whose dreams come true. Only, when art supplements and fixes the form, giving voice to the powers which reside in Nature, calling them forth to defined and determined uses, their efficacy is brought within the control of the human will as raw materials wrested from the bowels of the earth and fashioned for a purpose.

The power of the will and the intention of the soul are the main points in magic as in medicine. A man who wishes everybody well will produce good effects, while one who begrudges everybody all that is good and who hates himself may experience in his own person the effects of his poisonous thoughts.

That the *Magical* faculty does not rest with the good and virtuous alone we are well aware; for the *Magical Power* is inherent in every human soul, and has the power of acting not only immediately, upon bodies that are present to the sense, by means of the subtle powers of the eye and the breath, but also at a distance, upon bodies and persons more remote, by means of the desire and *phantasy* of the soul acting upon the vital principle within them. Recognize only that thoughts are things, creatures of life when animated by human desire, and in all respects obedient to their creator man, and what hinders that they should obey the behests of the soul, when sufficiently enforced by the impelling power of the will? Therefore, we may see that it is a motive alone which distinguishes good from evil in the use of occult forces. That which links the mind to its subject is thought; that which gives it form is imagination; and that which vitalizes it is the will. The will has no direct relation with motive, and may be used with equal power for good or evil. Will is but the vital or life-giving power to thought. Life has no qualities *per se,* though potential for all things; but it gains qualities by use or function. Motive determines the quality of our thought, inhering in and tincturing with its own nature every mental action. The motive is a power in itself, apart from the act, as the soul is a thing apart from the body, though expressing itself therein. Therefore causes that are brought into play by *Occult* means will differ in their ultimate effects by reason of the motive which ensouls them, though to the outward eye appearing in all respects identical.

Hence, to quote the words of a great *Adept,* "Whoever undertakes to govern and direct these mysterious powers, attempts a bold task. Let him consider well that he is penetrating, as far as is possible, into the highest laws of Nature. Never let him enter the sanctuary without reverential fear and the most profound respect for the principles which he endeavours to set in operation." Every person has this *magical* faculty within him, and it only stands in need of waking up. There is no limit to human perfectibility and power, and nothing which can be conceived of by the human mind that cannot ultimately be realized by man. Therefore the *Magi* have but four precepts:—*Know—Will—Dare—Keep Silent.*

CHAPTER III

EVIL SPIRITS

ACCORDING TO THE KABALA

The *Prince of Darkness, Beelzebub,* presides over nine orders of infernal spirits, according to the *Kabalists*. These spirits are the tempters of mankind. The *Occultist* affirms that they are the disembodied spirits of evil-minded men confirmed in wickedness by the perversity of their wills. Even presuming that they are no more than the evil thoughts and imaginings of embodied humanity, there is yet nothing, in a world where "thoughts are things," to prevent such from taking bodily shape and substance and thus, when stimulated by the force of men's evil desires, becoming active powers for evil.

Everybody has read of *Frankenstein's Monster,* that weird output of the imagination of the beautiful *Mary Shelley,* but few people have realized that the story embodies a great *occult* truth. It is perhaps not difficult to trace this creation of the daughter of *Charles Godwin*. One has but to study his work on *The Lives of the Necromancers* to be confirmed in the idea that what the father suggested the daughter elaborated in the laboratory of her own gifted mind. It was in the nature of a competitive essay, and gained the prize of publication. Study this story, and also the chapter on *"The Dweller on the Threshold"* in the popular novel of *Bulwer Lytton,* and you will have some notion of the experiences of those who are capable of creating, and thereafter of being obsessed by, the images of their own minds. *Will* and *Desire* created the universe. It should not be strange that it may create something equal to man when both the will and imagination of man are consciously directed to the process.

Of the *Nine Orders of Evil Spirits,* the first is that of *False Gods.* Here we have the concentrated worship and imagination of thousands directed to the same effect, the creation of *"gods."* We have knowledge of the *Saturnalias* and *Baldachinos,* the *Bacchanalias* and orgies of the heathen world. Such a god was that Satan who tempted the man *Jesus. Swedenborg* defines the difference between the satans and the devils when he says that the former apply themselves to the minds of men, instilling false doctrines and lies, blinding intelligence, stimulating pride and inciting to heresies and seditions; while, on the other hand, devils are such as apply themselves to the appetites, and by their affinity to the emotional faculty (whence they have their origin) seek to instil lust, greed, avarice, hatred, and every kind of illicit affection and perverted or depraved appetite. It may be well to accept this distinction.

The second order are called *Lying Spirits,* of which sort were those who obsessed the prophet *Ahab;* and over these is set a spirit called *Pytho,* who is the father of lies. These spirits apply themselves to the interiors of the vocal and respiratory organs by means of the brain centres. Some such are to be heard speaking through the mouths of persons entranced, such as *demoniacs, pythonesses,* and spirit mediums. Such an one is mentioned in the *Bible* as crying out in pain at the approach of *Jesus,* saying: *"What have I to do with Thee, O Son of David? I know Thee who Thou art!"*

The third order of evil spirits are those called *"Vessels of Iniquity"* and *"Vessels of Wrath,"* who are the inventors of all vices for the infesting of men and their ruination. Their prince is called *"Belial,"* who is without a yoke, being a renegade and disobedient spirit not subject to control. Of this order are the violent and lawless, murderers, and some suicides who kill themselves in frenzy. Of this order *St. Paul* speaks to the *Corinthians,* saying: *"What agreement hath Christ with Belial?"* For these spirits of *Belial* have no agreement with any, being, as it were, the *Ishmaelites* of the underworld.

The fourth order of evil spirits is called *"The Revengeful,"* their prince being called *Asmodeus,* who is the occasion of judgment. They were of the order let loose upon *Egypt* in the visitation by plagues, as recorded in *Exodus.*

The fifth order of evil spirits is called *"The Deluders,"* whose satan is called *Nahash,* the chief of those who have the spirit of the serpent. These cause signs and wonders and work all sorts of marvels in order to seduce men's minds from the truth. They are represented by the *Black Magicians,* the wonderworkers who seek to efface God and arrogate to themselves the power to control the spiritual world. In reflected degree they work through the minds of cheats, forgers and charlatans. That Satan who tempted *Eve* is of this order of the *Nahash* or *Serpents.* Of him it is said: *"He it is who seduces the whole world, doing great signs and causing fire to descend from heaven in the sight of men, seducing the inhabitants of the earth by these which are given him to do,"* as appears in the *Apocalypse.*

The sixth order is that of the *"Turbulents,"* presided over by *Meririm,* the *Prince* of the *Powers* of the *Air.* It is they who affect the air with tempests, corrupting the air with blights and poisonful exhalations, destroying crops and polluting the waters of the earth. *St. Paul* speaks of this *"Prince of the Powers of the Air."* These spirits have affinity with the thoughts and passions of men, and are evoked by the turbulence and passions of men's minds, as may be seen in great wars and revolutions.

The seventh order is that of "the Furies." Their Prince is called *Apollyon,* or in the *Hebrew Abaddon,* which means *"the Destroyer."* They are the cause of madness, frenzy, murders, massacres and intestine wars.

The eighth order of evil spirits is called *"The Accusers"* or *"The Inquisitors."* They are under the dominion of one called *Ashtaroth, i.e. "The Searcher."* In the Greek he is called *Diabolos,* or the *Calumniator,* and in the *Apocalypse* is referred to as "the Accuser of the Brethren, accusing them night and day before the face of God." For these spirits delight in persecuting the righteous, searching out their weaknesses and railing against them because of their imperfections. The common faultfinder is well within the category of those who owe allegiance to Ashtaroth.

The ninth order is that of *"The Tempters."* These are in close association with mankind, and one of their number is present with those who are in any way subject to the worldly spirit of greed and avarice. Their prince is called *Mammon, i.e. Covetousness.*

These nine orders of evil spirits are called *"transgressors,"* for they violate the commandments which in the *Hebrews* are but nine only, and not ten as commonly conceived: the first and second of the *"Decalogue"* being one only, and having reference to the worship of the true God and the sin of the making of false gods, whether subjective or objective; and Beelzebub is that supreme False God whom the sinful serve by error under whatever name it may figure.

MAN'S SPIRITUAL FREEDOM

To the end that mankind may be in freedom and reserve to itself the power to cast in its lot with the good or evil powers, these nine orders of *evil spirits*

EVIL SPIRITS

are, according to the kabalists, counterbalanced by a corresponding array of angelic orders. These are known as *Cherubim, Seraphim, Thrones, Dominions, Powers, Virtues, Principalities, Archangels,* and *Angels.* These Nine Orders are otherwise referred to as the *Metratton,* "they who stand about the Throne"; the *Ophanim,* otherwise called the Wheels of Life (referred to by Ezekiel); and the *Seven Planetary* Spirits, which include the *Archangels* and their hosts of subservient angels. These by their representatives are set over mankind for his government and well-being; else were man wholly abandoned to the machinations of evil spirits.

In the *Apocryphal* book of *Tobias* it is related that the *Archangel Raphael* did apprehend *Asmodeus,* and bound him in the wilderness of *Upper Egypt.* It has been thought that this story has reference to the presence of the planet *Jupiter* in the sign *Gemini;* for *Asmodeus* is of the sphere of *Jupiter's* evil spirits, and *Raphael* is *Mercury,* whose sign *Gemini* is said to rule over *Egypt,* and moreover it is the sign of *Jupiter's* debility. Ingenious as this interpretation may be, it appears to rest upon the association of *Asmodeus* with *Jupiter,* which may very well be the case, as *Asmodeus,* like *Jupiter,* is related to the office of the Judges; but it is not the fact, astrologically speaking, that *Gemini* rules *Upper Egypt,* but *Capricon,* or—according to the *Egyptian zodiac*—the *Crocodile.* Hence the *Egyptians* were called the *Mizraim* (those born from the crocodile).

Concerning the sphere of *Jupiter,* Hesiod says: "There are thirty thousand of the spirits of *Jupiter,* pure and immortal, who are the keepers of men on earth that they may observe justice and mercy, and who, having clothed themselves with an aerial form, go to and fro everywhere upon the earth."

No man could continue in safety, it is said, nor any

woman remain uncorrupted, and none could come to the end designed by God, but for the assistance given them by the benefic spirits, or if evil spirits were alone allowed to sway men's minds. Thus every man has a guardian angel and a good demon, as *Socrates* affirms, and likewise there are spirits of evil attaching to all in whom the passions are allowed free play; and these good and evil forces contend for the victory, the decision being in the hands of the man whose soul is the coveted prize. For man is in the middle ground of equilibrium, and freedom being allied to both the superior and inferior worlds by the dual aspect of his mind, being stirred by passion from below and illumined by intelligence from above, it is therefore in his will to whom the victory shall be given.

Therefore, we cannot impute evil to spirits that are by nature evil, neither lay our failures to their blame; nor accuse the benevolent spirits of any lack of zeal, seeing that it is by our own consent that this or that advantage is gained by the powers of evil. But the evil powers, once overcome, lose their influence over us in a great measure. And this is the meaning of the saying, "I will give you power to tread upon scorpions; nevertheless, rejoice not that ye have *power over the spirits*, but that your name is written in heaven."

Thus it is seen that evil spirits are compared to scorpions, and that they may be rendered ineffectual and harmless by the power of the celestial name, which is that spiritual or "new name" which is written upon the *White Stone,* as is said in the Revelations. The *Christ,* or Man made Perfect, is *Venus,* the Light Bearer and the Messenger of Peace, who gives his qualities to the overcoming of evil, and *"To him that overcometh I will give the bright and morning star."* Opposed to *Venus* in the spheres is *Mars,* the god of war, the promoter of strife and discord, the ruler of the *"Scorpions."* He rules over the eighth sphere and

EVIL SPIRITS

the eighth sign of the zodiac, *i.e. Scorpio,* which is associated with the *House of Death,* the terminal house of the natural soul. When good spirits and powers dominate this principle in man's nature—*i.e.* the *Scorpio* principle—there is the better hope of a deliverance from the evil of these spirits.

When it is said that *Michael* (the Sun-Angel) contended with Satan (*i.e.* Saturn) for the body of *Moses,* we understand kabalistically that the good and evil principles were in strife, *Saturn* contending that the body belonged to him by natural agreement, while *Michael* affirmed that he had redeemed it even from decay; for *Moses* was an Initiate of the cultus of *Ammon-Ra,* and his name denotes not only drawn forth and elected, but kabalistically he is nominated, for he was one of those named and appointed to a typical work.

This association of the spirits with man, and the sympathies and antipathies arising therefrom, is the reason that certain men are naturally friends or enemies of others.

A certain magician warned M. Antoninus of his friendship with Octavius Augustus, with whom he was accustomed to play, Augustus always coming off the conqueror. The magician, it is said, reprimanded Antoninus because he continued to consort with Augustus, although better born, more skilful and older than he, for, the magician continued, "Thy genius doth much dread the genius of this young man and thy fortune flatters his fortune, so that, unless thou shalt shun him, it appears wholly to decline to him." Thus it is that some men are brought to positions of preference and power irrespective of their individual merits, because the genius which directs them and presides over their fortunes is more powerful than that of their rivals. But the Genius of Fortune is not that of Life, nor that of Intelligence, these three being distinct: so that a man may become possessed of great wealth and die young, or show remarkable faculty without commensurate benefit. Therefore the Genius of Fortune and Life must be in agreement if the position is to be enjoyed, while that of the Intelligence and Fortune must be equally well disposed if the full reward of one's labors is to be enjoyed. Thus, all things considered, the choice must be in regard to that calling or profession which most suitably comports with the Genius of Fortune. This is taught in the horoscopical science, but otherwise is kabalistically determined according to names and numbers. These things, which have relation to the freedom of man, must be understood by those who would make election of times and seasons. It is good and proper to know whence benefits will be derived and whence evil will assail us; also those days, hours and seasons which are proper to our purposes, and those again which are incompatible; so that between that which is good and that which is evil we may so work that ultimately we may prevail.

CHAPTER IV

THE CAUSE OF DISEASE

In old times, when the teachings of Hippocrates were more in vogue than at this date, when *Aristotle* and *Galen* and *Ibn Sina* and *Paracelsus* made their contributions to contemporary medical science, it was the custom to regard man in terms of the cosmos. They classified all disorders in a comprehensive manner as accidental or incidental, as acute or chronic, as functional or organic. The functional powers were governed by the *Moon*, the organic constitution by the *Sun*. Accidental and acute ailments were ascribed to the action of *Mars*, incidental and chronic disorders to *Saturn*. *Mars* was responsible for all inflammatory action and fevers, while *Saturn* was the cause of all morbid diseases and loss of vitality. It was only a question of the distribution of the vital principle in man, and this, originating in the *Sun* and regulated by the *Moon*, induced fevers when in excess and morbid disease when deficient in any organ of the body. *Jupiter* was the great healer and arbiter of destiny, and it was his aid that the physician invoked when at the head of his prescription he wrote the symbol ℞—*Help, O Jupiter!*

This ancient custom, together with many of the terms of ancient usage, is retained by modern physicians, many of whom see no more in it than the letter *R*, the initial of the word Recipe. But we still speak of chronic diseases, while tracing nothing to the action of Kronos (Saturn). We own to a *solar* plexus and a *semilunar* ganglion, and there are many other terms which have survived the practice of putting new names to old facts when some new function or structural peculiarity comes under modern observation. Had the ancients known of the existence of *Uranus* they would have had a potent cause for paralysis, nervous lesion and similar disturbances of the organism, while in *Neptune* they would have found the cause of anæmia, consumption and wasting decline, and possibly of neurasthenia and the various effects of nervous depletion.

But who shall say, without making trial of the matter, that the ancients were at fault in regarding man as embodied *cosmos,* a compound of the free elements in the universe about him, or wrong in interpreting his various disorders in terms of the *stellar ambient?* It is, at all events, just worth notice that at the birth of *Miss Dorothy Kerin,* on the 28th November, 1890, the *Sun, Venus* and *Mercury* were in quadrature to *Saturn* and in opposition to *Neptune,* while on the 18th February, 1912, *Jupiter* was in the 13th degree of *Sagittarius,* the very degree of the *Zodiac* that was rising at her birth. The odds against this coincidence are 4,319 to 1. If it were a solitary example of what is said to be the beneficent influence of *Jupiter* in the saving of life it would not be so significant, but from the array of evidence accumulated by modern observations and retrogressive calculation, it is quite clear that the ancients were justified in their ascriptions in the case of *Jupiter.* Possibly it is not to the planetary orb itself but to the cosmic synthesis represented by it in our physical and mental constitution that appeal is made. Be that as it may, and while asserting the fact of planetary influence in human life without fear of contradiction I am not in a position to dogmatize as to the *modus operandi,* it is yet evident that there is a concert of action between the various cosmic centres and their corresponding principles in ourselves, such as to uphold the theosophic concept of man as *Microcosmos.*

I have just been speaking of cancer as a morbid disease. It was known to the ancients and by them named after that sign of the *Zodiac* which responds to the zone most frequently affected by the disease, namely, the breast and stomach. It has already been shown that *Saturn* was accounted the chief cause of disease. *Napoleon Buonaparte* died of cancer, and at his birth we find *Saturn* in the sign *Cancer* in opposition to the *Moon*. On the principle that one swallow does not make a summer, I leave the observation for what it may be worth, but it is satisfactory if we can recognize a swallow when we see it. We are on the way to distinguish between martins and swifts, and between house and sand martins, and thus forefended from building our house upon the sand. For although *Occultism* deals with an order of facts outside the normal range of orthodox science its methods are equally scientific, both analytical and constructive. If we take the *horoscopes* of a number of persons whose fatal illness was of the same nature and compare them, we shall find a factor that is common to them all. The existence of this factor in the *horoscope* of a living person is a presumptive argument for *"tendency"* to the same disease. If in event that person develops the particular malady indicated by the horoscope, we have at once a scientific basis for a system of astro-therapy and a valid means of prognosis.

Assuming that the *astrologers* have been as busy in their special department of research as have the representatives of other branches of learning in theirs, it may reasonably be expected that with an equal body of tradition behind them and an equal field of experimental research before them, they have arrived at conclusions of which they are as sure as any scientific man can be in regard to any matter. To ignore their statements or to disparage them without test appears to me to be wholly prejudicial to the interests of truth and most likely to reflect upon the scientific integrity of those who pursue either course, for as the old philosopher says: "Where confidence is lacking it is not met by trust."

PSYCHOPLASM

In regard to the faculty of *auto-suggestion* in connection with *psychotherapy;* it has been suggested that this faculty depends on the activity of the subconscious sphere of the mind. It is seen that all action is either purposive or automatic. All purposive action tends to become habitual, and to the extent that it becomes so, it passes from the region of *mind-control* into the subconscious region where it is capable of itself controlling the mind. We then recognize what is called the *"force of habit."* But it is further suggested that the activity of the subconscious part of the mind-sphere is at its maximum when we are asleep, whether natural or hypnotic. Certainly it is a fact that at a particular stage in *hypnosis* the subject passes out of the power of the *hypnotist* to control and assumes an activity of mental function which is remarkable both as to range and precision. But the facts seem to suggest something more than mere automatism, for while the patient remains subject to suggestion there is evidence of something more than the discharge of accumulated impressions. The subject is not found to be blundering about in the lumber-room of the mind, searching for odd bits of stuff that will answer the purpose in view, but is seen to exhibit direct perception of things as they are, the power to traverse space and to annihilate time, and to come into voluntary and conscious relations with the past and the future as if they coexisted and had a present reality. Many cases are on record. A single well-attested case would have sufficed.

These facts are given for they are very closely akin to the teaching of the *Adepts*. It is that the mind-sphere or soul is divided into two hemispheres, one of which is on the level of normal consciousness and the other below it. The *nous* or mind is then seen to be energized from above by the *pneuma* through inspiration, and from below by the *psyche* through instinct. Intuition and instinct, or inspiration and passion, are thus at opposite poles of the mind-sphere, and appeal can be made to either by suggestion through the sphere of the mind. We trace these opposite aspects of the mind in the *Oversoul* and the animal soul of the mystical schools, the *augoeides* and *antinous* of the earlier teaching. In the *Yoga* system they are the *Buddhic* and *Kamic* principles, the centres of spiritual knowledge and of animal desires respectively, the process of *Yoga* being to bring these opposite poles of our nature into active accord.

There are on record a fairly large number of instances in which it appears that either one's subliminal consciousness or an extraneous intelligence affords prescience of things in which one is not particularly interested and for which there is no special call. Persons have thus been given the winning numbers in lotteries without, at the same time, being given the means of participating in the benefits attaching thereto. An instance quite pertinent to the general accusation of futility lodged against this class of intelligence came to my notice on the 2nd of April, 1912. A lady, on awaking that morning, exclaimed, *"Number twenty-nine will win!"* Asked as to whether it was a number in a lottery she at once replied: *"No, it's a horse."* Some cudgelling of brains failed to suggest any means by which the information could be applied. The problem was, however, successfully solved by a twelve-year-old girl who took the morning paper in hand, counted from the first name of the opening event in the programme for the day, exhausted the names in that event and continued into the second event until she arrived at number 29, against which was the name *"Primrose Morn."* Obviously it had no connection with the 2nd of April, but on reflection it was remembered that the lady was born on the 29th of the month and was engaged to be married on *Primrose Morn.* Immediately below this name in the list of competitors was *"Marie's Choice,"* and the lady's name is *Marie.* The coincidence was completed by the winning of the *Bestwood Park Plate* by *"Primrose Morn."* Reference to the morning papers of the 2nd of April last will enable the reader to check this statement. The rising and bursting of these bubbles of subconscious activity appear to be quite automatic and in most instances without purpose or utility. They serve, however, to demonstrate the fact that there is such a source of inspiration, a submerged selfhood in touch with the *anima mundi* or world-soul, upon which we can at all times call for information and aid. The purpose of *Occultism* is to put us in the way of doing this when and as we please. From the point of view of the world-soul, the future and the past are coexistent. Every race is already run, every event is historical. This gives a new and a higher meaning to the old saying: The future is only the past unfolded. As the old Philosopher says: *Tsae yin jo fang*—all truth is paradoxical.

Another interesting feature of the *psychic* principle in us is that of the projection of the ethereal double or wraith. It is recorded of *Goethe* that he had a vision of himself, or rather of his double, on more than one occasion. It is well known that he had the faculty of exteriorization of thought, the projecting of visible thought-forms, in a remarkable degree. This faculty of *Kriyas'akti* is cultivatd by the *Yogis* of *India,* and forms an important feature in all *occult* training. The poet *Shelley* frequently effected "exteriorization" and was seen by *Byron* and *Trelawney* and by his wife on more than one occasion to be visibly present when it was certain that he was some distance away from the scene. Many such cases are on record. I know a *Yogi* in *India* who has been certified to be visibly present in four places at the same time. Even allowing for slight errors of observation in regard to time, the fact is remarkable, especially as there had been no suggestion of pre-arrangement. The theory of *"expectancy"* would not therefore cover the ground.

A *disciple* of mine sends me the following certified experiences of psychic self-projection—

"I intended visiting a great friend (who is psychic *when* I am with her), twenty-five miles away, from Saturday to Monday. On the previous Tuesday night I could not sleep at all; still wide awake at 3 A.M. I suddenly thought of Miss H——, and instantly was in her dining-room, in thought, saw vividly furniture, etc., and felt beside me her dear dead mother (my friend). I thought we both went upstairs together to the 'spare room' I usually occupy when visiting. We went into the room, and I walked straight to the window, held the curtains back with my hands and looked out, then turned and looked at the bed, surprised to find Miss H—— in it, instead of her own room; turned to the door and came out of my 'brown study' to find myself in my own bed at home.

"When I visited her on Saturday she said: 'About 3 A.M. last Tuesday I wished you in your own home; I slept in the spare room that night for a change, and could not sleep; I felt you and my mother were downstairs, and distinctly saw you both come into the room. You went straight to the window, parted the curtains with your hands, and looked out, then turned your head and looked surprised to see me in the bed and walked out of the room.'"

Now, I had said nothing about my "psychic visit." Yet in every detail it was authenticated at the other end!

One night I dreamed I felt nervous (it was a brilliant moonlit night), and that I would go into the next room and see if M—— was awake for company. I went in my nightdress, barefooted, and distinctly shivered with cold. I found M—— sound asleep, so did not awaken her. Wondering what time it might be, I walked to the mantelpiece, where she keeps her little clock; *it was not there,* but on a chair near the bed. I made out fifteen minutes past something, but the moon was not now so brilliant I thought. Then feeling very chilly, I dreamed I returned to my bed. I awoke with a shock (the shock of returning to my body?) feeling sure I had *been* there. My watch pointed to 4:15. My body was perfectly warm, so it could not have been sleep-walking; it was very frosty. Next morning at breakfast I said: "Where do you keep your little clock?"

M—— said: "Usually on the mantelpiece, but it is a good way from the bed these frosty mornings, so last night I put it on a chair near my bedhead."

She also said: "I had a curious feeling when I awoke this morning that your presence had been in my room during the night."

These experiences undoubtedly show the power of the human mind to take form and to effect visible self-presentation at a distance. It is presumptive evidence for the existence of a mind-form or *karanasharira,* which if temporarily separable from the physical centres of consciousness, may be so separated permanently at the moment of death, and thus assume independent and conscious existence in a world inhering in its consciousness. While affording *a priori* argument in favor of a reasonable belief in post-mortem existence, it does not prove immortality. The two cases stand upon entirely different grounds and require distinctive evidence. I know that after the butterfly has emerged from the chrysalis it has independent existence and that it is neither grub nor chrysalis, but a potentiality that has become realized in a new order of being. But I also know that the butterfly comes to an end. Our problem is concerned with the soul of the butterfly and what becomes of it thereafter. The case is not identical but merely analogous. The human evolution is presumably a good many stages beyond that of the *lepidoptera*.

Yet I find it quite the usual thing, especially among *Spiritualists*, to regard evidence of *post-mortem* existences as equivalent to evidence for immortality. *Occultism*, in common with all the great Religions, teaches that *post-mortem* existence is natural and imperative, while immortality is spiritual and conditional. If the shell of a nut be broken the kernel will continue to exist as nut for a considerable time. It is thus with the *psychoplasm* after separation from the physical body or shell. It is said of those who have attained: These are they over whom the *second death* hath no power. The tendency to regard all that is not physical as being spiritual in its nature and constitution, is one of the greatest fallacies to which modern interpreters of psychic phenomena have contributed. A change in the sphere of activity does not involve change of character, nor does it determine the degree of spiritual consciousness of the individual. That is a matter of evolution, of knowledge and devotion. The confessed ignorance of discarnate intelligences upon matters mundane and spiritual is sufficient evidence of this fact.

CHAPTER V

PSYCHOMETRY

THE EXISTENCE OF A SUBTILE AURA

A MODERN dictionary gives to *Psychometry* the following meaning:—"*The occult power of divining the secret properties of things by mere contact.*" This definition will serve if we render its terms somewhat more explicitly. *Psychometry*, then, is a little known or understood power, claimed by some experimenters in unfamiliar laws of nature, by which not only the secret properties of things may be determined, but by which a train of events associated with an object may be discovered, or interpreted.

To give an example: a *psychometrist*, to whom has been handed, in a sealed outer cover, a letter, will endeavor to reproduce the emotions which influenced the writer when composing it; to portray his personality, and the cause which determined his action; the immediately preceding events connected with the inception of the letter; and the relationship his personal surroundings bore to current events and persons. The train of *"causality"* progresses from particulars to universals. Or it may be that a weapon, associated with a crime, is the subject of investigation. It will then be the task of the *psychometrist* to reconstruct all the details of the crime itself, the motives which were responsible for it, and the determining incidents which led up to its execution. The attempt to demonstrate the probability, or even possibility, of this power may seem futile to the materialist. In attempting the demonstration we will first briefly review the position of modern science in its theory of "force."

"Force is that which changes, or tends to change, a body's state of rest or motion," in its kinetic aspect. There is also the static form in which "passive forces" are postulated. These act independently of motion. A force is said "to do work" actively when changing a body's state of rest or motion, and passively when resisting such changes. Energy is "the capacity for doing work," of which there are many forms, the principal being chemical, electrical, heat, sound and light. Further, it is stated that if energy in one form is used to do work, the work done, in its turn, produces an equivalent amount of some other energy. For example, if electrical energy be used for chemical dissociation, the work done will again reproduce the energy used, in another form, such as sound, light or heat. This is the necessary conclusion of the dogma of the conservation of energy. By the further admission that the ultimate state of matter, as *"electrons"* or *"ions,"* is nothing but static charges of electrical energy, associated with ether, modern science practically admits the conditions necessary for establishing our case for Psychometry. The *Occultist* has his own hypotheses respecting the origin and formation of matter, but as we are more particularly concerned here with *"force,"* we may exclude the nature of matter as inessential to the discussion in which we are engaged.

To make clear the ground it is desirable, however, to reassert that modern science admits that anything which causes or tends to cause a change in a body's state of rest or motion, is a force. My purpose here is to demonstrate that thought is a force. Now, some schools of materialistic science somewhat dogmatically state that thought is a function of matter. And matter, they tell us, quite as dogmatically, is essentially inert. That is, matter cannot move of itself. It must be acted upon by a force in order to change its state of rest or motion. The movement of the brain cells, it is said, gives rise to ideation, to thought. The materialist, however, is on the horns of a dilemma. For though he says that thought is a function of matter, before he can obtain thought he has first to posit motion, and his two fundamental postulates are matter and motion. Thought, then, must be correlated with one or the other. The materialist himself would admit that thought is not material. That it is not matter. And if not matter, it must be motion. It cannot be anything else, since, to the materialist there is no other but these two ultimate concepts. If, then, thought is correlated to motion in its aspect as force, it would appear that it is thought which causes the movement of the brain cells, or, more accurately stated perhaps, thought is the movement of the brain cells.

Occultism takes up a definite position. It agrees, broadly, with the postulation of the two fundamental concepts of modern science. It regards the manifested universe as subject to a law of periodicity. There is an out-breathing which culminates in gradations of matter as the outer clothing of gradations of force. The essence of matter and force is one. To our senses, it is manifested as two facets of the one substance. Underlying it as its primal cause are ideation and will. On the physical plane—the normal plane of objectivity —it postulates an ultimate state or condition of matter. This is homogeneous, impalpable and imponderable. None of the properties of matter as we know it are apparent. It would correspond, broadly, to the hypothetical ether of science. But matter to the occultist exists in various planes of objectivity which interpenetrate one another. To the lowest in order is related the material or physical plane of science on which the gross earthly body of muscle, sinew, bone, tissue and flesh functions.

At the termination of a great period of manifestations, an enormous astronomical cycle, the visible universe ceases to exist as a world of objective form. It becomes once more formless and impalpable, returning for a time to its original essence, once more to reawaken to activity. The philosophical conceptions of Spencer in his cosmography are not widely remote from the truth as seen by *occultism*. Motion is the one reality. It is that which ever is, and was, and will be. It is the ever becoming. And motion denotes life. Life indeed is but a complex of motions: molecular, metabolic, atomic and electric, even to modern science. The latter professes itself unable either to account for the origin of life or to explain its deprivation from some spheres. *Occultism* postulates life as eternal and infinite. In its highest aspect, life is pure motion. Nothing in the universe, on any plane of action or manifestation, is without motion, and therefore motion or life is the inherent property or quality of matter. There is no dead matter. The atom is instinct with life—with motion. The corpuscles and ions of modern science—the ultimate particles to them —are to *occultism* worlds in miniature.

Motion, then, is life. And thought is motion. Thought, then, is a living force: a moving cause. Thought is that which can change a body's state of rest or motion. Thought causes the motion—it is the motion—of the brain cells. And behind thought lies the will of which motion is the external expression. This is why, then, it is said that to the forces known to physical science, occultism adds another, the most Indeed, in its sublimest aspect, it is the prime cause of all—the "will," of which "thought" is the materialized expression in the phenomenal world.

74 THE CAVE OF THE ORACLE

"Thought," then, is a form of energy, inasmuch as it possesses the capacity to do work. The thought-suggestion of the hypnotist—whether verbally uttered or not—will do work on the subject. In the annals of orthodox science, in the French hospitals, the thought-suggestion has been shown as "chemical energy" in producing anæsthesia, and in other instances as "heat energy," when a burn—an erosion of living tissue—has resulted from the unuttered thought-suggestion of the operator. Other cases might be cited to demonstrate still further the fact that "thought" is a form of energy, as real as light or electricity.

Thought may well be compared with light, as an undulation of the ether, or to electricity, by virtue of its capacity, as "energy," to create a stress in matter. Like other forms of energy, when it does work, the work will, in its turn, produce an equivalent amount of another form of energy. Light travels in all directions, and with almost inconceivable rapidity. So also does "thought," impressing itself similarly, by its etheric undulations, upon all bodies within its range. When such bodies absorb "thought-energy," work is done by the stress which is created, and this work will reproduce in its turn this, or another form of energy. To return from this necessary, lengthy digression to the concrete example. Ideation must precede the will to act. So far as the actions of the writer of the letter, or the perpetrator of the crime, were premeditated, their previous "thoughts" would have been impressed, not only upon the articles specified, but upon every other object within range of their meditations. The thoughts being so impressed, set up a state of stress, and this "work done" has the capacity to produce an other form of energy by transformation.

Light, in acting upon a photographic plate, produces a stress which, when suitable means are employed, reproduces itself as chemical energy in dissociation of the silver-salt. Thought being the most vital and energetic of all forms of energy, all bodies are assumed to be more or less amenable to a stress in consequence of its action. It may be assumed that the lapse of considerable time will serve to dissipate this energy by infinitely small gradations of release of the stress. A photograph, fading, in the course of years, may serve as a rough analogy. When the necessary means of transforming the stress is provided, by the presence of the psychometrist, it is suitably released by this "re-agent." This may be further explained by reference to the photographic action of light. In this latter art the essentials for the reproduction of a picture are as follows: a sensitive plate, an exposure to concentrated light, by means of a lens, and a reducing agent to render the "latent image" produced by the exposure, visible.

In *psychometry*, it is held that all bodies are more or less sensitive to thought. That thought, whether conscious or unconscious, acts upon them, as light concentrated upon a sensitive plate does, and produces upon them a *"latent image."* Their sensitiveness probably depends in a measure upon relative proximity to the locality of the sources of energy, in the same way that the light rays, impressed upon the plate, are those only which are reflected by the objects within the camera's range. The latent image, psychometrically, is made visible or audible, by an agent capable of disturbing the *"stress"* which occasioned it. The "conscious thought" of the operator acting, like the developer in photography, upon the latent image, transforms the potential or passive energy, into kinetic energy, the energy of motion, *i.e.* sound or light. The etheric vibrations thus released are presented to the inner senses of the *psychometrist* as *"ideation."*

This theory also implies that any other object other than those instances, if present at the time, would enable the *psychometrist* to reconstruct the scene. A succession of mental pictures is given, in which all that is essential to the reproduction of the events is included, but overlaid and obscured by the other multitudinous impressions associated with the object, which have not yet been dispersed by time. The skilled psychometrist has to dissociate, and delete all other impressions than those essential to the purpose.

So far, one aspect only of *psychometry* has been dealt with. Another phase of this *Occult* science is the ability to diagnose the properties of bodies, substantially present, but shrouded.

Here again it is urged that nothing but the extended action of natural laws is exhibited. Light, sound and heat are vibrations and undulations, in a scale which apparently exposes numerous "*gaps*," above, below and between. Gaps to which our normal physical senses fail to respond. These "*gaps*" are, however, only apparent because the vibrations they represent are inappreciable to us. For example: a sound may either be so low in pitch, or so high, that it is inaudible, but the vibrations are virtually present as "sound" though we do not hear it. So with light. Above and below the series of undulations which are capable of "*impressing*" our optic nerve are millions of others to which we are insensible. Science, with its instruments of physical research, demonstrates the existence of these "*invisible*" light rays. The "*ions*" and "*electrons*" of the atom of a fragment of gold, or of the atom of carbon contained in a lock of human hair, are in a state of inconceivably rapid rotation and vibration. These vibrations give rise to undulations in the ether. May it not well be that some human organisms possess organs of sense, analogous to our normal physical organs—possibly but an extension of them, or their functions, on another plane of consciousness—capable of responding to these more delicate stimuli? In this hypothesis lies the justification of *psychometry,* and modern science certainly does more to substantiate than to controvert its claims.

But it may be thought that, though it may be easy to suggest the presence of such senses, it would be difficult to afford any proof of their existence. It is necessary, then, to investigate the principles of man as postulated by occultism. Reference has already been made to the lowest plane of objectivity—the physical plane of modern science—to which is correlated the physical body. Interpenetrating this is what the *occultists* call the *astral* or *etheric* plane. Modern science, in one of its dogmas, says that no two atoms on the psychical plane have ever been in actual contact. If this is so, how does this exact science explain sensation? What are touch and taste? It would be difficult, we think, to explain them on the older basis of physics which accepted the atoms as the ultimate particle. But now that modern science believes that matter is not "matter" at all, it comes virtually into line with occultism. For the latter has all along taught that the material particles of science were transient and accidental aggregations of finer substance built into a web of *etheric* material, so to speak.

It is this web of etheric material which forms the bridge for sensation, which is communicated to the grosser particles of the physical body as stresses. The *etheric* body, the impalpable and imponderable but delimiting structure, is the vehicle for receiving, in the first place, the stimuli from outside. This body has its organs of sense corresponding to the objective organs of sense of the physical body. These sense organs are hypothetically postulated, but are demonstrated by dream phenomena, by the subliminal consciousness, and by the *hypnotic phenomena*. The infallible memory is associated with these sense organs, and the subconscious mind is one of its expressions.

Normally these senses do not function for us consciously. That is, our consciousness works only on the lowest plane of all—that of the physical body. In abnormal individuals there is a functioning, of sorts, on this astral or etheric plane which is semi-conscious only.

In *psychometry*, these etheric senses are in part awakened. Semi-consciously, sometimes unconsciously, the elementary *psychometrist* becomes aware of impressions received, he or she does not know whence or even how. But as the faculty is awakened the will stirs the consciousness, which is then carried over to another plane of being and action. It then begins to function as a child does, haphazardly and almost blindly, till it learns by experience to use its newly acquired powers. But there still remains to be acquired the capacity to bring back the knowledge thus obtained.

A rough analogy would be that of the hypnotized subject. In the *hypnotized* condition the etheric senses of the subject are stirred by the operator. The subject is seen to be actually conscious on a higher plane of being—on the plane of the sub-conscious mind. But when awakened, the subject is unable to recall the experiences related by himself, for example, to the operator, when in the *hypnotized* condition. The capacity is not present to bring over on to the ordinary plane of action and consciousness the experiences of the etheric plane. But occultism is in general agreement with the teachings of the laws of evolution. On the physical side it admits the ascent of man from more primitive types. It also postulates a continual ascent for man to a spirithood, and eventually to godhead and omniscience. Further, it lays down most emphatically that there are even now immense differences in mental and spiritual growth. That there are now with us men and women who represent what the general stage of growth mentally and spiritually will be for the race millenniums hence.

It is, then, these etheric senses which will, when they come to be used generally, carry the race forward on another stage of its journey. It will render man practically independent of our three-dimensioned space. It will open out to him records which have been stored etherically and invisibly for him. The impress, the impacts, so to speak, of thoughts upon so-called inanimate objects will be within his range of developments. He will be able, by his astral or etheric senses, to reconstruct the scenes which have passed into the endless cycles of eternity. And he will also be able to construct the future which is the outcome of the law of causation. For the future is contained in the eternal present. There is no dead matter. There are no inanimate objects to the *occultist*. All is life. All is movement. All is an ever-becoming. Death signifies and connotes changelessness. And there is nothing unchanging. Nothing is imperishable save space, motion and the root.

Modern science agrees with these dicta. For space is inannihilable: motion, the cause of energy, is eternal, and the root, matter in its ultimate aspect, is indestructible. It is only the form of matter and the rate and direction of motion that varies. Form is continually changing. Its change posits motion. And motion is life. Matter, then, as form, is the manifestation of life, and the impact, on all matter, of force, as thought, is the cause of its change of state. The change of state may be, frequently is, only a static change. It needs development to convert it into a kinetic change.

To perceive such changes the finer instruments of the etheric senses are necessary. The power to carry the knowledge thus obtained over to the waking consciousness of the physical plane is obtained by the application of experience precisely as in the realm of any other domain of science. Changes of state, the expansion of a body by the applicatoin of heat energy, are only perceptible by the trained operator with the necessary instruments to record and measure such changes. But modern science would not deny that such changes happened because it had not the means to descry them or to record them.

Psychometry is concerned with just such changes. The *occultists* say such changes take place. They describe the instruments by which such changes are observed. They translate with practical application the bearing of such changes. They do this on lines acceptable to modern science. There is neither transgression nor transcendence of natural law. There is merely an extension of the principle of natural law into a field just beyond the present range of physical science.

Psychometry asks only for an impartial hearing in its own interests. It neither begs for favors nor asks for a packed court. It is conscious of its own strength to withstand the test that science with its own hypotheses can apply to it. But it enforces its demand to be tried. It insists that it cannot be dismissed as an idle chimera, because, forsooth, science cannot measure the length of a thought with a foot-rule, nor weigh it in a balance. Modern science must remember that the spring balance, the gramme weight and the foot-rule are equally indeterminate in ascertaining atomic weight, the velocity of the alpha-rays, or the frequency of the etheric undulations of light.

AURIC EMANATIONS OF OBJECTS

THE trained *Occultist* is capable not only of manifesting intense psychic activity under the direction of his will, but also on occasion of maintaining a perfect passivity which enables him to receive and register impressions of a subtile nature from the external world and to give free play to the subconscious side of the mind-sphere.

The *psychometric* sense is that by which we receive impressions coming to us imperceptibly through the sense-organs. The functions of this sense imply not only the existence of a subtile aura attaching to every material object, but also the ability to perceive the effects produced in ourselves by attention to the auric emanations of such objects.

The *Occultists* affirm the existence of an aura to every solar system, to every planet of that system, and to every person or thing upon that planet. This *aura* is a plastic sensitized medium of an etheric nature, which interpenetrates and extends beyond every material body. It is the storehouse of every experience attaching to the body it is related to. A piece of rock will thus preserve to us not only the record of the earth of which it is a part, but also the individual record of its detached existence; and this will be the case with every minutest particle, in less degree of intensity, of any body whatsoever. The greater the mass the stronger will be the auric emanation. In the case of the molecule, the aura would seem to correspond with the heat-sphere; but unlike the aura, the size of the heat-sphere will depend on the elasticity of the atoms composing it, and this again on the activity of its electrons.

The aura which surrounds the earth has been called *Alkahest*, "the *Astral Light*," and the *Memoria Mundi*. It is the universal library of fact and fiction to which every sensitive, every writer, every inventor, every occultist, has conscious or unconscious access. Not only does it contain the record of all that has happened in the world, but also all the thoughts that have been projected from men's minds, and all the plots and schemes and glorious ideals which have found place in the imaginations of sinners and saints the world over.

This recording film, this cinemato-phonograph, is capable of reproducing its records or rather we are capable of perceiving them, wherever the faculty of *clairvoyance* or *clairaudience* is developed to a sufficient degree to be able to penetrate beyond the riot of auric emanations by which we are continually and immediately surrounded. But even without either clairvoyant or clairaudient faculty, we may contact this emanation by the *Psychometric* sense.

It is inferred from the conditions under which *Psychometry* is practiced that the range of this sense is not comparable with that of either *"clear"* seeing or hearing. In the exercise of the faculty it is necessary to have some object such as a letter, a lock of hair, a glove, belonging to the person concerning whom inquiry is made.

This object is then held for a short while between the hands of the *psychometrist* or *"Passive"* and sometimes it is raised to the level of the forehead and placed between the eyes.

If the Passive is sufficiently sensitive to get *en rapport* with the subject, there will arise before the mind's eye a series of pictures or scenes, or yet only vague apperceptions of form, color, distance, locality, time, etc. These must nevertheless be at once communicated by word of mouth to a Recorder, however detached and irrelevant they may appear. The mind of the Passive must be kept entirely free from speculation, reasoning or guessing. If the automatic faculty is allowed free play it will inevitably lead to correct impressions after it has been allowed a certain amount of free exercise.

When it is considered how seldom in daily life this subconscious self is allowed to function, it is hardly to be wondered at that a faculty which has lain dormant since childhood should, upon being aroused by the will, take occasion in the first place to stretch its limbs and gather its forces. Give it opportunity and time in which to carry out the behests of the Will, and it undoubtedly will prove itself a faithful servant.

The psychometric sense is in all respects analogous to that exercised by the passive *seer* in the act of *crystal-gazing* or *"scrying"*; only it does not necessarily or generally extend to vision, but rests in a certain apperception or "impression" which takes no definite mental form.

There are, moreover, certain difficulties always to be encountered in the exercise of psychometry. *"Clouding"* may result from a state of incomplete rapport, which does not always rest in the degree of sensitiveness enjoyed by the Passive. It may well be due to the fact that the glove or article submitted for contact has not sufficiently strong associations with the person to whom it belongs. A letter, for instance, has frequently but slender association with the writer of it, while it is saturated through and through with the magnetism of the recipient owing to its having been long carried about by him.

"Overlapping" may arise from cross-influences, as when an article, long in the possession of one person, is given as a memento or keepsake to another, and then is submitted for contact by the Passive. In such case the whole of the later associations have to be waded through and obliterated from the test before the information sought concerning the original possessor can be arrived at. Meanwhile, the psychometric sense is becoming tired and blunted in its perception, so that little that is to the actual point of inquiry may be elicited at first. In a second or third test from the same article the familiar surface ground will be traversed more speedily and there is then every likelihood of a satisfactory conclusion.

"Obliquity" may very easily result from the error of applying remarks concerning one set of impressions

to the wrong person. Thus if I go to a Passive to make an inquiry about a person named *A*, and take with me an article which was at one time in *A's* possession, but has some time been held by me, the Passive may very well be voicing some valuable information about myself while I am erroneously trying to apply it to the subject of my inquiry, namely *A*. Until therefore the Passive has given some unmistakable indication that he or she is on the track of the actual point of inquiry, care must be exercised in the interpretation or application of any remarks that may be made.

It is usually found that the best results are obtainable under conditions of complete isolation both physical and mental. If the mind of the Passive is troubled about his own affairs or is laboring under the least degree of physical discomfort, there will be a surface-ripple or superficial disturbance of the mind-sphere which will effectually prevent the Passive from getting down to those still, mysterious depths of consciousness in which the secrets of the ages lie hidden.

"Misinterpretation" may occur in cases where the *clairvoyant* faculty lends itself to the *psychometric* and evolves a symbolic figure by way of expression.

Thus I was once asked to *psychometrize* an envelope taken haphazard from a packet of papers then in the possession of a physician at *Madras, India*. On applying the envelope to my forehead I was presently affected with a sense of distance and some degree of giddiness. The inference was that I was in contact with conditions which implied estrangement, loss or obscuration, and that the position referred to was an elevated one either physically or spiritually. Following on this immediate perception I saw a black vault like an ebon sky in which flamed a comet. This passed away and nothing more was seen or sensed. I suggested that the comet was a stranger to the system, implying a person of wandering habits, one who had distinctive merits or a certain celebrity—a possible "cynosure for wandering eyes." And then comet—from Latin *coma,* the hair—was there any suggestion there? Assuredly there was, for on disclosure I saw that the envelope contained a lock of black hair which I was told was that of *Damodar K. Mavalankar,* a young student of *Occultism,* who had been fired with an ambition to go to *Tibet* and who last was heard of from *Darjeeling* before crossing into *Tibet.* Involuntarily there sprang to my mind the words of *Tennyson:* "And some of them have followed wandering fires, lost in the quagmire." In some few minds there still lingers a belief—or it may be only a hope—that the pilgrim will one day return.

Another instance of a more direct sensing owing to the illumination of the symbolic element, was afforded me by a lady who had an eye to the value of test conditions. This lady handed me a box of some three inches cube, wrapped around with a paper which was tied and sealed. On holding this in my hands I presently perceived a wide flowing landscape of undulating fields on which were cattle grazing. I remarked with interest that they were of milky whiteness. On the neck of one of superior proportions a bell was hanging. I heard this bell ring, and from that point I gathered no other impressions save that the country to which this scene belonged was *Greece.*

On opening the package at request, I found it to contain the box first mentioned, and within, securely packed and stuffed with soft paper—the identical cow-bell of which I had received both *clairvoyant* and *clairaudient* impression!

Providing the student is willing to be perfectly honest with himself and frank with others, there is nothing that should prevent him from acquiring a mass of first-hand evidence of the existence and exercise of this *psychometric* faculty.

I would particularly recommend a reading of THE GREAT BOOK OF MAGICAL ART, HINDU MAGIC AND EAST INDIAN OCCULTISM, as being one of the earliest and most convincing of the many works extant dealing with this subject.

DOWSING

The *psychometric* sense is very clearly displayed in the process of water-finding by means of the hazel-rod, called *"Dowsing."* The following account of some successful experience of this sort will prove of interest.

"A few weeks ago," says the *Westminster Budget* of December 1893, "there took place some operations with the divining-rod by *Mr. Stears*, of *Hull*, who was called to *Mr. S. Campion's* farm at *East Hesluton*, near *Malton*, to search for a water supply. At that time he marked two places near the farm-house where, he said, the presence of water was indicated by the rod. Since then *Mr. E. Halliday*, plumber, of *Malton*, has bored an artesian well at one of the places indicated and found a plentiful supply of water at a depth of 87 feet, after going through sand, clay and a bed of what Mr. Halliday says is quartz and lead ore. *Mr. Campion*, who was previously without a supply of pure water, is delighted with the results of the visit of the diviner, and has faith in the power of the rod. These and other experiments were conducted in the presence of *Julia Lady Middleton*, the *Hon. Geoffrey* and *Mrs. Dawnay*, *Lord Middleton's* agent, and others. *Mr. Stears* also claims to be able to locate minerals as well as water, and affirms that not one person in ten thousand can use the rod successfully."

I do not know how Mr. Stears arrives at his figures, and I do not suppose that one person in ten thousand has ever attempted to employ the faculty. As a fact well within the experience of students of *Occultism*, and fully illustrated nearly a century ago in a book called *Welton's Rod,* it serves but to enforce the fact that the *divinatory* faculty extends to all the senses, including that of sight, that of hearing, of smell, of touch, and even, as here, the nervous sense of feeling, which is not the same as touch, but is an *auric* sense extending over a very wide area.

As yet, however, the majority of people are oblivious of the fact that such psychic faculties exist, and even those who possess them and have them in something like working order are conscious of having but little control over them. The functions of the higher senses are as yet imperfectly understood. Every sense has its octave, but the involuntary functioning of any "sense octave" is apt to be regarded as a sign of insanity by those who have no knowledge of the psychic faculties. Even genius has been related to insanity and *Lombroso* and *Nordau* have sought to prove genius is often a form of insanity. It should rather be regarded as an exaltation of faculty which relates its subject to a plane of consciousness removed from one's normal experience by some degrees. Thus while new centres of activity are being opened up, and are as yet under imperfect control, whole areas of the brain are left in neglect. Hence, to the casual observer, genius is not distinguishable from some incipient forms of insanity. The eccentricity of genius is one of the most significant indications of the functioning of the subconscious part of the mind. In just the same way the opening up of new centres of activity in the psychic nature of man is frequently attended by temporary loss of control over the normal brain functions. Loss of memory (amnesia), *hysteria, absent-mindedness, unconscious utterance* of one's *thoughts, illusions* and *hallucinations, irritability,* indifference to one's surroundings, spasmodic muscular actions and similar eccentricities, are among the products which signalize the evolution of the newly-acquired psychic faculty. These symptoms will, however, subside as soon as the new faculty has been established. Nature is jealous of her offspring, and all her forces are concentrated in the process of generation. The abnormalities incident to the period of gestation clearly prove this. Once her end is attained, however, she resumes her normal functions. Those who aim at the development of psychic faculties must therefore be prepared to pay toll to Nature, according gladly whatever she demands by way of tribute.

"The universe is thine. Take what thou wilt, but pay the price."

And what is the price of *seership,* of the *divinatory* faculty, of any of these superior gifts of Nature? *What is it worth to oneself?* That is the price we may be expected to pay.

CHAPTER VI

DREAMS AND VISIONS

According to the *Adepts* of *"The Eastern Order Of Sacred Mysteries,"* which has its headquarters in *Northern India,* the states of consciousness are primarily threefold: (1) *Jagrata,* or waking consciousness; (2) *Svapna,* or sleeping consciousness; and (3) *Sushupti,* or spiritual consciousness. That which is normal to the dream-life is *svapna.* It is convenient to regard the ego or conscious individual as a thread (*sutrâtma,* the thread-soul, as the *Hindus* call it), upon which is a bead representing the centre of consciousness. If the thread be divided into three colored sections, we shall then have the three planes of life upon which the centre of consciousness can function. In the present instance we are concerned with the middle stage or plane, that of dream-life. There is a neutral or nodal point separating each of these stages of consciousness from that above it. As regards the mass of people, the *jagrata,* or waking consciousness, is the norm. But in *mystics* and visionaries the *svapna,* or dream-consciousness, is the *norm,* and just as the ordinary, matter-of-fact person passes in sleep from *jagrata* to *svapna,* so the visionary to whom *svapna* is normal, passes in sleep to *sushupti.*

This being understood as the concomitant result of variety of evolution or individual development as distinguished from mere intellectual accomplishments, we may next consider the nature and cause of sleep and then pass to a study of dreams, their nature and significance.

During the activity of the body during the day every muscular action, every mental effort, is followed by the breaking down of a number of minute cells all of which discharge their vital contents into the system. This vital content of the cell is called *devâna* by the *Adepts*. It is like an electrical charge. So long as it remains in the cell it can be used and directed at will in the form of a current of energy, but when the cell is broken up the force is dissipated into the free ether of space, and goes to swell the sum total of latent energy in the world. When this process of breaking down has gone on in the system for some time, the body is flooded with the vital principle, and if this were to go on to any great extent, disease and death would be the inevitable result. Vitality is not to be measured by the amount of the *devâna* in the body, but by the amount of it we have under our control. *There is a good deal of life in a putrid carcase, but none of it is co-ordinated or under control.*

For the purpose of reabsorbing the vitality and repairing the cellular structure of the exhausted battery, *Nature has provided that exhaustion shall be followed by sleep; as day is followed by night and summer by winter.* When the powers of recuperation become impaired, when this subtile Archæus passes beyond our power of automatic refreshing, then age and disease begin to assert themselves.

Ad rem.—We sleep because we are exhausted; we awake because we are refreshed. When we are asleep we dream, because the immortal soul of us, that which we call the Man (*manas*, or mind) never sleeps, since it is never exhausted, and this transference of its activity and of its dual functions to a higher or more interior plane of consciousness is the cause of dreaming.

Of what nature, then, are dreams? Obviously they are only the perceptions of the soul in its middle or twilight state of consciousness. Dreamland is shadowland, neither darkness nor pure light, but a *chiaroscura* of mingled perceptions. Dreams are primarily of three kinds:—

(1) Those which arise as memories of the waking state of consciousness; (2) those which have their origin in the current changes of thought and feeling taking place in the dreaming state; and (3) those which descend as illuminations from the superior plane of spiritual consciousness.

These three kinds of dreams may be called the memory dream, the phantastic dream, and the clear-dream. They are related to the physical, psychic, and spiritual principles in man.

The transition from one stage to another is called mutation, and the sleeping condition is then known as the higher or lower mutative sleep. The following diagram shows the various stages of consciousness:—

Every kind of dream is in some measure illuminative, for even though the dream may consist entirely of our memory-products, it is the selective faculty of the soul which, taking a little here and a little there, fashions the fabric of a dream and builds up the mosaic from the multitude of detached experiences. The dream thus presented to the mind is reflective of a state of existence which is interior to that of the waking perception and to that extent instructive to it. Excessive or indiscreet feeding will cause disturbed dreams, nightmare and a sense of oppression, and this instructs us that even though mind forms matter, it is certain that matter conditions mind, and that undigested or unassimilated food, which would hardly trouble the wakeful mind, becomes a source of impediment to the soul that would willingly spread its wings were it not hindered and restrained by its care for the body. A good tenant cannot go away upon a holiday leaving his house in disorder, for should he do so it would be a constant source of anxiety to him. It is right that he should find it clean-swept and garnished at such time as he would again take possession.

The greater number of dreams are of this psycho-physiological nature and origin, and must chiefly be interpreted in relation to the body or those mundane events which bear upon the immediate personal interests of the dreamer.

Dreams that are disconnected from the physical senses are in the nature of soul images, for the soul thinks in symbols and understands by natural interior perception of their significance. Hence, frequently the allegorical or symbolic dream carries with it to the waking perception a sense of its true significance. All true dreams can be interpreted by natural correspondence, and anybody who is versed in symbology, not as an archæological science but as a soul-language, can interpret dreams. But in order to apply such interpretations to the individual dreamer it is necessary to know to what order in the sidereal world such individual may belong. In so far as the individual is reflected in the horoscope of birth by means of his physical *persona*, it becomes possible to use the astrological key for the interpretation of dreams.

To many people *flowers mean sickness,* while to others they signify joy and festivity. A probable explanation of this difference lies in the fact that certain persons are in the habit of being visited with gifts of flowers during illness, and there is hence an associated idea of flowers and sickness; while others not so fortunately placed as to be recipients of floral condolences have only associated flowers with the brightest days of their lives, for flowers belong to the summer days and to the country, where leisure and rest are usually sought.

In similar manner names have a distinct significance when closely associated with events of our waking life.

DREAMS AND VISIONS

Thus I know a lady to whom any name with the syllable NOR in it is disastrous; and *"Normanhurst"* was lost by her through an unfortunate financial crisis; *"Norma"* was the name of a fine pedigree St. Bernard dog that died from pneumonia brought on by careless exposure while the animal was with the veterinary surgeon; *"Norsa"* was the name of a ship christened by her which went down on its first voyage; *"Norland"* was the name of a place in which her child was rendered speechless through a fall; and I regard this as sufficient reason why, without being able to ascribe any reason for her prejudice, the name of Nora puts her on the defensive whenever she meets a person of that name. The soul in the dream-state instinctively surrounds itself with the images of those things, their forms, colors, names, which in waking experience have been associated with happiness whenever its interior state is a happy one; and, on the contrary, when its unclouded perception of the future is fraught with prognostics of evil import, it throws down upon the brain of the sleeping personality the images of such things as, within the experience of that personality, are associated with danger or hurt to mind, body or estate. With such solicitude does the soul watch over its physical instrument that it will forewarn it of any danger that is likely to befall it providing the conditions for conveying and registering such a message are present.

Similarly the Spirit of Man watches over its Psyche, or female counterpart, and in clear dreaming conveys to it that degree of spiritual instruction or admonition which it is capable of receiving or of which it has present need.

This Spirit has its own imperishable vehicle, the solar body, into which the soul or lunar body is merged after the death of the physical. The solar body is called the "golden bowl," the holy grail; the lunar body or thread-soul is called the "silver cord," and the physical body is called "the pitcher" and the vessel of clay. Thus in *Ecclesiastes* we read: *"And desire shall fail, because man goeth to his long home, and the mourners go about the streets: or ever the silver cord be loosed, or the golden bowl be broken, or the pitcher be broken at the fountain."*

These things are necessary to be known before we can attempt to regulate our knowledge concerning the nature and origin of dreams.

The symbolism of dreams has therefore a three-fold application: a material, a psychic, and a spiritual or mental. We call that spiritual which arises in the mind from the illumination of the spirit, that psychic which arises from the emotions, and that physical which has its origin in material experiences. The spiritual dream is distinguished from the psychic by its being unattended by any degree of emotion as doubt, anxiety, trouble or fear; but only a sense of great beatitude, the mind being detached from the vision and regarding it as a magnificent spectacle. The psychic dream, on the contrary, is attended by a distinct emotional disturbance, and if the dreamer does not actually take an active part in the scene as one of the *dramatis personæ,* it at least identifies itself sympathetically with one of the actors and experiences by repercussion just as much as if it were taking an active part. What a mother feels for her child in joy or sorrow, in pleasure or in pain, the Psyche feels for the images of its creation, for they are indeed its children. It is a rare, but nevertheless certain, fact that men experience in their physical bodies that which they have been dreaming. Thus I have recently read of a man who dreamed that he was lying upon the sands exposed to a burning sun, and on awaking he continued to experience the burning sensation in his face, and going to the mirror discovered to his vast astonishment that his face was actually and most thoroughly sunburnt. This phenomenon is known as astral repercussion.

I once saw the wraith of a living person walk into the room where I was sitting in company with others, and it was observed that the wraith, which appeared in all respects a figure of flesh and blood and properly clothed, knocked his head against the projecting corner of a wardrobe and instantly disappeared in thin air. The next morning the person whose wraith we had seen appeared with his eye bandaged up and explained that he had a bruised swelling and must have been stung in the night by a mosquito. We, however, told him a different story.

"Artists and students have frequently obtained instruction in their dreams regarding things which they desired to learn. The imagination was thus free and commenced to work its wonders. It attracted to it the *Evestra* of some philosophers, and they communicated their knowledge to them.

"Such occurrences frequently take place, but it often happens that part of that which is communicated is forgotten on awaking to the outer world. In such case it is necessary to observe strict silence, not to speak to anybody, nor to leave the room, nor take any note of things; but to eat nothing and remain still; and after a while we shall remember the dream.

I have found that if, on awaking from a dream part of which is obscure or forgotten, I continue in the same position, keeping my eyes closed to all external things, and then go over the dream in my imagination, the missing part is generally restored, as if I had dreamed the dream all over again. Every one knows how readily a disturbing dream may be dispelled by changing the position of the body. It is sometimes more convenient to change the position of the mind.

The astral life is most active in man during his

sleep. The sidereal (solar) man is then awake and acts through the *evestrum* (or astral body), causing occasionally prophetic dreams, which the person will remember on awaking. But there are also elusive dreams, caused by other influences, and man must therefore use his reason and discrimination to distinguish the true from the false.

There may be more reliance placed in dreams than in the revelations of the *necromantic art;* because the latter are usually false and deceptive, and although the elementals which use the *astral bodies* of the dead on such occasions will give correct answers to questions and often confirm their assertions with oaths, yet no implicit confidence can be placed in what they say because they do not wish to speak the truth nor are they able to speak it.

"Therefore the patriarchs, prophets and saints preferred visions and dreams to any other method of divination. . . . Supernatural dreams take place at times among the present generation, but only the wise pay any attention to them. Others treat them with contempt, although such dreams are true and do not deceive.

"There are some people whose natures are so spiritual and their souls so exalted that they can approach the highest spiritual sphere when their bodies are asleep. . . . Dreams, visions and omens are gifts of the sidereal man, and not of the elementary body. . . . The elementary body has no spiritual gifts, but the sidereal body possesses them all. Whenever the elementary body is at rest, the sidereal body is awake and active, because the latter needs neither rest nor sleep; but whenever the elementary body is fully awake and active, the activity of the sidereal body is then restrained, and its free movements are impeded or hindered like those of a man who is buried alive in a tomb."

A man who is content with the rushlight of his own reason will hardly welcome the effulgent rays of the universal sun. What benefit can such people derive from the most perspicuous dream?

Localization of dreams is a very remarkable phenomenon. Yet almost all persons have some select spot, some haunt to which they repair from time to time in their dreams. It is always the same place and thoroughly well known to the dreamer, though quite outside all waking recognition. At such places one meets the same persons, and the dream is continuous of that which preceded it. For many years I had such a place where I met and discussed with one whose name I afterwards saw in an old Italian book of biographies, and since then I have not been able to revive the experience in my dreams. But I know that in some cases these localizations are retrospective and are reminiscent of a former life, while in others they are prospective and have reference to a place and environment which will eventually be known in experience.

The interpretation of dreams is an art that is known to the wise Adepts. Many books proposing to interpret dreams have appeared from time to time, but from their contents it is readily seen that they are designed to impress the ignorant reader or to express the ignorant author, for by no rule of art or understanding of universal symbolism (which is the only language known to the soul of man) can the interpretations be justified.

The present work does not permit of a thorough exposition of the symbolism of dreams, and it is not therefore thought advisable to attempt the task of formulating a system of interpretation. Such a syster, however, does exist and has been reflected in all the scriptures of all peoples from time immemorial. The universe and man are consentaneous. There is an universal symbolism, an universal language, and—if you please—an universal *Dream-book*. But this same book needs reading.

VISIONS AND THEIR INTERPRETATIONS

THE passive or *direct vision* is presumably a representation of the actual state of things perceived, whether relating to the past, present, or future. The circumstantial account given by the seer is sufficient to indicate that it is a direct vision.

The *symbolic vision* is, however, fraught with many difficulties for those who are unacquainted with symbolism and the method of interpretation. Something, therefore, may be said on this point.

Symbols are thought-forms which convey, by the association of ideas, a definite meaning to the mind which perceives them. They depend entirely upon the Laws of Thought and the correspondence between the spiritual and material worlds, between the subject and object of our consciousness.

Among the ancients, symbols were the original form of record, of communication, and of writing. The *hieroglyphics* of the *Egyptians*, the word-pictures of the *Mayas* of Central America, the *ideographic* writing of the *Chinese* are all forms of symbolism derived from natural objects. The *Hebrew* alphabet is quite symbolical. Any letter speaks to us of the nomadic people who were *"dwellers in tents."* Such names as *ox, tent, tent-door, tent-peg, camel, fish, fish-hook, eye, hand, basket, rope-coil, ox-goad, water,* are names of letters which cannot fail to convey an idea of the primitive *Semites*. They are all names of natural objects, and they are all symbols. Bring together the letters *yod* (hand), *daleth* (tent-door) and *oin* (eye), and you have the word *yedo*. The hand denotes action, power; the door, an entry, initiation; the eye, sight, perception,—liberally, opening the door to see; ideographically, knowledge. Similarly, in *Chinese* the words for wall, face, and man, when brought together as a symbol, indicate a wall-facing man, by which we understand a prejudiced and bigoted person, one who will not see or enlarge his horizon.

All symbols may be interpreted by their known natures, qualities and uses. Thus an *arm* will signify defence, power, protection; a *mouth* speech, revelation; an *ear* news, information; if distorted, scandal, abuse. The *sun* prosperity, life, honours; the *moon* crescent, prosperity, increase, improvement; when gibbous, loss, decay, decline. The *sun eclipsed*, death of a man; the *moon eclipsed*, death of a woman; *bread*, food, sustenance, knowledge, preservation; and these are all natural interpretations. Every symbol has reference to the Three Worlds, the physical, intellectual, and spiritual, *i. e.* to Nature, Man, and God.

If the question be concerning the material world, a ship as a symbol would show commerce, trade, a voyage, good or bad according to the condition of the ship; as if in full sail under a clear sky, prosperity is signified; if in distress or with flagging sails, an unfortunate condition is signified.

If the question has relation to the intellectual world, the same symbol would denote the interchange of ideas, good or bad news, etc.; if to the superior world, the same symbol would denote that communication with the spiritual world is increasing or decreasing, as the symbol may indicate. A pirate ship might thus refer to plunder, slander, infringement of rights, or death.

Symbols are almost infinite in number, and the interpretation of them requires unprejudiced skill, but they are nevertheless an important subject for study, and the use of the Crystal or Mirror by a positive seer can hardly be beneficial without a profound understanding of this subject.

Although every symbol has some general signification in agreement with its natural qualities and uses, yet it obtains a particular meaning in relation to the individual. This is also the case in dreams, where every person is a natural seer. Few, however, pay that attention to dreams which their source and nature warrant. The *Crystal* is but a means of bringing the normal dreaming faculty into conscious activity.

No definite rule can be laid down as to the interpretation of visions, and the seer or seeress will be found the best interpreter. Yet the differences of meaning, whether in dreaming or visions, of any particular symbol is of common experience. Thus to dream of a naked child imports trouble to some people, while others have a standard dream of wading in water whenever trouble is to be faced. To dream of butcher's meat means financial troubles to some people, while to others it imports gain by speculation.

The controlling factor in this matter is probably to be found in the constitution of the psychic and mental faculties of the seer as expressed in the nativity. A great deal may be said for a system of interpretation that has for its basis the dominion of the signs of the *Zodiac* at the birth of an individual and also the horary positions of these signs at the time of the visions or dreams as the case may be.

It may serve in some part to illustrate the foregoing remarks if I here recite some experiences which have come within my knowledge and have been either witnessed by me or have been the result of my own exercise of the faculty of induced clairvoyance. Being of a positive type of mind, and not normally *clairvoyant*, the visions have chiefly been of a symbolic character.

A lady friend came to me in June 1896 and asked me to gaze in the *Crystal* for her, as her mind was much exercised on a certain point. In due course she was told that she would hear news from abroad concerning the birth of a child in some hot country; it would be a boy, and would arrive in the month of February of the following year. This was not at all what the lady was inquiring about, although I had no means of knowing what was in her mind as no intimation of any sort had been given to me by her. Nevertheless, she did hear such news, and in February 1897 a boy was born to the lady's sister in India.

I next told her that on a certain date, while travelling, she would meet with an accident to the right leg. On that day my friend actually slipped between the platform and footboard while getting into a train and suffered severe abrasion of the shin of the right leg, together with serious muscular strain from which she suffered for several days.

It was further said that this lady would hear some good news concerning her son in connection with papers and a contest. This was to happen in the month of October, and at that time her son passed his examination for the military college with honours.

As an illustration of the direct or passive vision, the following is of interest:—

Mrs. H. the seeress was consulted by a lady of some ability in a special line of literature, though this fact was not within the knowledge of the seeress. The lady was told that she would go up a staircase into a dingy room with a roll of papers under her arm. She would see a dark man who was thick-set and of quiet demeanour. The man would take the roll, and it would be a source of good fortune to her at a later date.

These circumstances were literally fulfilled by the lady taking a manuscript to a publisher, who accepted and published it. The description of the man was quite accurate, as I who know him can testify.

These two cases will serve as illustrations of the two orders of vision, the symbolic and the literal. The symbolism of the former case not being recorded, however, but merely the interpretation and its fulfilment, it will be of interest to cite another instance in which the symbolism is preserved:—

Vision.—A public square is seen in which was the effigy of a lamb mounted upon a pedestal. A flash of lightning is seen to strike the image, melting off one of its ears. A Catholic priest came along and pointed at the figure.

Interpretation.—A member of the community to which the consultant belonged would thereafter be converted to the Roman Church.

Fulfilment.—By the next mail the consultant learned that such was the case, an important member of the body having gone over to the Catholics as predicted.

Vision.—A man is seen dressed in black, wearing the habit of a judge. He holds some papers which he endeavours to conceal beneath his robe. He appears unsuccessful. The papers are too large. A snake is seen at his feet. It rises up against him.

Interpretation.—A certain man who is indicated by his profession will be guilty of obscuring the truth and of misrepresentation. He will be the subject of criticism from a source that is not suspected.

Fulfilment.—The man conspicuously indicated had followed the legal profession. He was convicted of having issued misleading and fraudulent testimonies with intent to deceive. Criticism led to inquiry and conviction.

Vision.—The same man is seen lying on a bed. He is *in extremis.*

Interpretation.—The man so indicated will be cut off by death three years from this time.

Fulfilment.—His death took place by strangulation due to a throat affection exactly three years from that date.

It is not always conspicuous from what source the seer derives his interpretations. We have to remember that the condition in which the seer voices his predictions is a psychological one, whether natural or induced, and in that state natural symbols take on a very different significance to that which they would hold in the normal waking consciousness. It is similarly the case with dreams. They may be perspicuous and natural, or wholly symbolical. The influence they have upon the dreamer while asleep bears no sort of relation to their significance to the waking consciousness. How pregnant with meaning and how important and real they appear in the dreaming, only to dissolve into ridiculous triviality and seeming nonsense the moment our wide-awake reason is brought to bear upon them! It would appear that between the visionary and waking states of consciousness there is a complete hiatus, so that even the laws of thought undergo a change when the centre of consciousness is removed from the inner world of thought and feeling to the outer world of sense and action.

Not infrequently the visionary state is induced by excessive emotion. Some persons of peculiarly sensitive nature will fall into the clairvoyant state while engaged in deep thought. This is akin to the "brown study" when "a penny for your thoughts" is likely to prove a good investment if you are a student of psychology. In such cases the thread of thought appears to be broken and a vision, wholly unrelated to the subject but a moment ago in the mind, suddenly appears to usurp the field of consciousness. It is as if the soul of the sensitive, while probing the depths of thought, suddenly comes into contact with the thin partition dividing the outer world of thought from the inner world of knowledge, the domain of doubt and reason from that of intuition and direct perception; and, breaking through this partition, the soul emerges into the field of light beyond. A rapid alternation of the centre of consciousness from the dream or psychic state to the waking or normal state will, if sustained, assuredly bring about the phenomenon known as clairvoyance. Swedenborg claimed to have been simultaneously conscious in two worlds for days together. But the centre of consciousness cannot be located in two places or states of existence at one and the same time, and it may therefore be said that the alternation was exceedingly rapid and continuous, giving the sensation of being thus divided in consciousness. I have myself experienced this condition both experimentally and naturally, and at such times it would be impossible to say whether I was in this or that of the two bodies, one corporeal and the other ethereal, through which I was conscious of functioning.

CHAPTER VII

OMENS AND ORACLES

Divination by *omens* and *oracles* is one of the oldest of the *occult* arts. Like *Astrology,* it has been, in some periods of historic time, upheld by the State, and officially practised in its interest. The *College* of *Augurs* at *Rome* will occur at once to the classical student. He will need, perhaps, less reminding of the prominence of the oracles in the Grecian epoch. A little further back we have the *Egyptian oracles.* To-day, in the extension of our knowledge of anthropology and folklore, we note how widespread has been the practice of observing omens and consulting oracles in almost every phase of intellectual growth.

Astronomical phenomena were the basis of astrological science. The separate incidents were noted as omens; as portents generally of evil. Man in his primitive state was obsessed with fear. Hence his prognostications were usually of woe and distress. As he grew in knowledge and learned to conquer the powers of nature, he was enabled to see in unusual happenings the indications also of good fortune to come. Dreams and apparitions were held to be of profound significance. Though many dreams might have been accounted for by aberrations of the physiological processes, there was a residue in which indications were given of future events. That such is the case to-day, no serious student of psychology denies. The instances are too many, and too well vouched to be explicable on the score of coincidence. Dreams, then, formed an important factor in the field of omens.

Dreaming itself is a passive function. The faculties are not normally exercised in dreaming. Two points arise from this consideration. Because volition is not exercised in dreaming, the experiences are frequently not sequential, nor orderly. As a result it was found that it was necessary to have an interpretation of the dreams if their significance was to be fully understood. Hence arose the need for divination by seers who would explain the import of the dreams.

Thus it is seen that though dreaming itself is not an occult art any more than mediumship is, divination, for purposes of interpretation, is an *occult* art. The materialistically inclined will perhaps say that the seeing of apparitions and visions are merely a day-dreaming. "Such stuff as dreams are made of" readily recurs. But this is to beg the question now, when it is generally scientifically admitted that dreams, even, are an indication of consciousness on another plane of being. The student of psychic processes sees in dreaming a real functioning, though this may be mostly aimless and inconsequent. There is usually, too, an extreme difficulty in bringing over to the waking consciousness the result of the astral perambulations.

This is not unreasonable. We should not expect a child of quite tender years to be able to reconstruct and relate its experiences of travel through strange lands and contact with strange peoples. It would have hazy notions of dimly perceived differences. But these would be inchoate and unreal to it by comparison with the solidity of its normal surroundings. And so it is with dreams. We are children of tender years. Our astral senses are imperfectly awakened to the perceptions. Our notions are dim and hazy. And when we recall them at all it is as a mere confused mass of impressions which we disperse as idle chimera.

But there comes a time when the visions are no longer blurred, indefinite and confusing. They assume sharply defined characters and lines. There is an intensity of impression that carries the ideas clearly over into the waking consciousness. There is an actuality and a reality in the perceptions which will no longer be denied. The child has grown. The senses are attuned more accurately to the vibrations. What is seen and heard is understood and takes form accordingly. The astral senses are awakening to the new world in which the wanderer has blundered and stumbles. *"Behold I dreamed a dream."*

It was held, for ages, that dreams, or dream visions, were sent from above as warnings. It was the simplest form of communication between the *Divine* and His creatures. The ordinary mortal could not face directly the glory of the *Divine*. Its voice could be heard and its mandate given only when shrouded. Its supreme refulgence was too great for direct approach. The full vision would have been too awful to withstand. So, in the old scriptures, man was warned in a dream. Or when an apparition was necessary, the *Divine* took shape of lowlier mien. An angel appeared—*Jacob* wrestled with the angel. Later there were the burning bush, the cloud by day and the pillar of fire by night. Dreams and apparitions were the forerunners of omens and *oracles*. Perhaps the first instance recorded of the former would be the voice of the *Spirit* as He walked in the garden with His threat of evil as the punishment for man's disobedience.

Prophecy, both sacred and profane, was more akin to omen than to oracle. The essential difference between them would appear to be that an omen is unsought. It occurs, and its meaning has to be assigned. The *oracle,* on the other hand, is consulted when it is desired to read the future. Omen and oracle are complement and supplement. The *oracle* was devised to supply the blanks left by omens.

The prophets of old were leaders of the people. By

their apparent capacity to read signs and portents; because of their ability to read the future and direct the movements, social, moral and political of their flocks; leadership was tacitly given them. They spoke out of the fullness of their knowledge. They communed with the oversoul. They were enabled to observe and read the signs which were not seen by others. They constructed a view of the future from the higher vision accorded them. Their astral senses were awake. They used the knowledge thus gleaned to advise and abjure the peoples they led. And from their prophecies arose a record which time has justified over and over again as if to confuse and confute beforehand those who would deny the possibilities of such foreknowledge.

And so long as modern thought confined itself to the realm of the purely physical, to that which could be weighed in the balance, or measured in velocity, it was incredulous and condemnatory. But now that the psychical is at least receiving attention, and the physical has receded over the borders of ethereality, justification is at hand for prophecy.

Omens may be roughly divided into two classes, particular and general. In the former are to be found those which, while not applicable invariably to a single individual, are yet of a personal character. The spectral coach, which is reported to drive up to the door of a North-country mansion and presages a death in the family, is one. The white bird of the *Oxenhams*, which has given warnings for generations, is another. The *Banshee*, of Highland tradition, which is heard by members of the family as a summons to one of them to prepare to depart, is a further instance of the particular case of omens.

Allied to this type of omen is that of the luck of *Edenhall*, the statue of *Pallas* at *Troy*, the coronation stone of *Scone*, and the *Ancile*. Each of these possessions, whilst it was retained in the hands of those who owned them, assured them of success But their loss or destruction presaged disaster. When the wooden statue of *Pallas* at *Troy* was stolen by the *Greeks* the city was reduced and fired. The removal of the coronation stone to *Westminster* carried with it the succession to the throne of Scotland. Rome fell when its *Palladium* was lost.

A well-authenticated case of personal omen is that of a family in which, three days before the death of a member, a dirge-like strain of music is heard in the air. This, according to tradition, has been observed for centuries. One member of the family who had heard it himself twice, and noted the accuracy of its forebodings, attempted to discover its origin.

It appeared that in the twelfth century the head of the family took with him to the crusades his youngest and favourite son. The son was killed in battle. The father lamented his untimely and unprepared death. So great, indeed, was his grief that, returning to England, he entered one of the monastic orders. His purpose was twofold. He desired to spend the remainder of his life in prayer—first, for the repose of the soul of his son; secondly, that in future no descendant of his should meet his fate without due time for preparation. For years his most intense desires were concentrated upon the fulfilment of his purpose.

The *occultist* would explain the result by the formation of an agency with nature spirits, or elementals, which would persist for untold generations, by virtue of the activity and intensity of the thought power poured into the astral atmosphere. The form of the agency was of no concern to the pious crusader. He was intent only that his warning should be heard. As thought is a persistent force, or mode of energy, it was concentrated with the elementary powers and is liberated now as occasion arises. The direct descendants of the old crusader hear again the strains of martial music which was the dirge in *Palestine* seven hundred years ago.

Many similar cases could be cited. And it would probably be found that most of them are explicable on the same lines. The records of the great families teem with these personal warnings or omens. However absurd it may be considered is the apparent credulity of those who take them as warnings, they have the justification to urge that they work. The warnings are generally true prognostications. And what more could one ask?

But quite apart from these individual and personal indications are omens of general significance. These are multifarious. The breaking of a picture cord, the violent slamming of a door, when there is no draught to cause it, breaking a mirror, stumbling or falling, the crossing of the path by a black cat, the creaking of furniture, the appearance of an owl or its screeching, the flight or fighting of birds, spilling the salt, howling of dogs, ear-tingling, all are general omens of various import. These are general omens which are known to most Western peoples as popular superstitions.

Each land has its own variants of their significance in detail. But there is a striking similarity and agreement almost on the main points of the values of each omen. It would seem that there has been either a common source from which such knowledge or myth has been derived, or that there is some underlying principle to which they may be referred. It would be difficult to justify the former proposition,—and not much less so, perhaps, to elucidate the truth of the second.

In *India*, the land of *magic* and *mystery*, omens form no small part of the religious beliefs of many of the peoples. For *India*, be it remembered, is an agglomeration of races, nations and tribes. In no other part of the world, possibly, are we able to trace such profound distinctions in language, customs, economics and morality. But underlying it all is the dependence upon omens. Reference is made in the *Hindu* classics to omens associated with quiverings and throbbings of the body. A quivering of the right eye indicates good luck. A quivering sensation in the right arm is believed to denote marriage with a beautiful woman.

In offering animal sacrifices, a practice still maintained in many parts of India, the movements of the animal before the slaughter are carefully observed. A very liberal interpretation is placed upon the slightest movement. A voluminous list of *omens* is given, both good and bad, as observed in *Malabar*. Crows and pigeons, moving from left to right, and dogs and jackals moving in the reverse directions, are accounted good. Screams, cursing, sneezing, a stool carried with its legs upwards, or a cup or dish carried with its mouth downwards, is bad. The worst of all omens is allowing a cat to cross one's path. On New Year's Day, the effect of *omens* is believed to last for the ensuing year.

If a winnow slips when winnowing rice, or the oven gives vent to a hissing noise, the arrival of a guest is foreshadowed. If a light goes out during meals, it is an evil omen. If a traveller sees a hare on his way he will not succeed in the object of his journey. When a child sneezes the bystanders wish it long life. Eclipses are periods of evil. *Comets* are also evil omens. A third wedding is considered to be of evil import amongst the *Brahmans*. If a *Brahman*, therefore, desires to marry a third wife, he is first wedded to a tree, the arka plant. The third wife then becomes his by a fourth marriage, and so the evil omen is averted.

There is a *Tamil* proverb relating to the selection of a wife, to the effect that curly hair gives food, thick hair brings milk, and very stiff hair destroys a family. *Omens* in connection with child-bearing and birth are numerous and curious. The birth of a Korava child on a new moon night is an omen that it will have a notorious thieving future. If a dog scratches the wall of a house it will be broken into by thieves. A dog approaching a person with a bit of shoe leather augurs success. If a dog enters a house with wire in its mouth, the master of the house must expect to be put in prison.

The hair marks on the bodies of horses and oxen, formed by the changes of direction in which the hair is growing, called the crown, ridge or feather mark, form the criterion of its value. The positions indicate whether the animal will bring luck or not to its owner; an animal is rarely kept which has unlucky marks.

It would be well-nigh hopeless to attempt to give a specific explanation of each of the omens to which reference has been made. It must be sufficient to try to prove a general justification for them. But first it is desirable to refer to the degradation of idea which almost invariably occurs with the lapse of time, and by the passage of a notion, orally, through successive generations. *As a platitude, the saying that there is no smoke without fire is hard to beat.* And its most useful analogy, perhaps, is that there is no myth without truth. The foundation of all myth is doubtless historical fact in every instance. But so distorted and overloaded does it become, that it is sometimes difficult to trace its origin or to recognise its validity.

So with many *omens*. Starting with an actual occurrence, possibly with a tragic effect. Phenomena occurring concurrently with or immediately before the happening were ascertained to have something to do with its causation. The connection at times quite conceivably may have been remote. But like circumstances being thought invariably to produce like effects, it would be recorded amongst the wise ones that such things were of evil import.

In other words, the basis of the belief in omens is experience. And, lest it be urged by the dialectical that superstition might be similarly defended, let it be said at once that this is equally true. The grossest superstition has its origin in fact. It may be difficult to deduce the fact from which it arises, but it is nevertheless true that the most absurd—apparently—superstitions have actually arisen in this way.

Witchcraft, sorcery, and magic, to mention three only of what it is common to call superstitions, are now known to all serious students to have a very real basis in natural, but frequently perverted, powers. There is no supernatural. The supernormal there may be, and is. The piety which believes in the miracles of *Christ,* and the bigotry which ascribes sorcery to the devil, are not far wide of the mark.

A better understanding of the underlying principles of the universe has shewn how futile were our previously limited concepts. The supernormal tends constantly to become the normal. The boundaries of the physical plane are being pushed outwards. We begin to sense the psychical, the ethereal, the mental and the spiritual planes, which lie beyond it and behind it. We begin daily to realize that the physical plane is a mere cloak, that it is but a garment of manifestation, for the powers which reside beyond its valuations, to use for their projections.

There is no breaking of the natural laws in miracles. There is but the extension of those laws in a supernormal exhibition of the ultimate spiritual energy which is the essence of the universe and the cause of its appearance. The stilling of the storm, the resurrection of the body, the thousandfold reproduction of the loaves and fishes, are marvellous exhibitions, but are not even the transcendence of natural law. They are explicable by the dicta of modern science. They are not to be reproduced by Tom, Dick or Harry. But they are neither impossibilities nor distortions of facts. They are simply revelations of the mastery of the higher principles over the lower forms which depend upon them.

Matter, that wonderful sheet anchor of physical science, is in the last analysis only the ether in motion. The physical atom is the universe in microcosm; within it resides an almost unbelievable store of energy. It is, in fact, just a centre of energy.

But thought, the servant or vehicle of the will, is another form of energy. Hypnotic phenomena shew this to be so. The physical is subservient to, dependent upon, the psychical. The tiny magnet of the school child will lift a little piece of steel or iron, weighing a few grammes. The modern electrical generator, the huge alternating machine, will hurl at a tremendous speed masses weighing a million times as much. The principle is the same, the power is identical. It is only a difference in the quantity of the energy used. The thought, then, which will induce a muscular contraction in the limb of the hypnotized subject is capable too of producing meteorological changes; changes in the polarity of the atoms of the human body; dissociation of material bodies; association of material bodies.

Man, essentially, is a dynamo. But usually he acts as a motor only. Rarely is he dynamic. He is respondent rather than originative. He is a standing example of the physical convertibility of electrical machines. They may be used, by the application of current to them, to produce mechanical motion. By the application of mechanical motion to them they may be made to produce electrical energy. In his response to the grosser influences man is the motor. He gives out mechanical energy only.

By linking himself up with the basic spiritual force

of the universe, he becomes capable of output of vast stores of electrical energy. He becomes dynamic. He shews a potentiality for good or evil of immense range and almost inconceivable power. The *Christ* was just such a dynamo. By virtue of His association with the Father, the typified over-soul, as the vehicle of the ultimate spiritual energy of the universe, He was able to manifest that power in various ways. His was the gigantic system of electrical alternators which could produce a storm as easily as still it, which could dissociate His own body or cause it to appear, as readily as He was able to multiply, to produce, in fact, bread and fish from the ethereal world stuff from which all materiality arises.

Omniscience bears to supernormal premonition much the same relation that the alternator does to the child's magnet. All men are potential *Christs*. But the day of entering completely into their kingdom is afar off. Many, however, begin to shew signs that the gulf is not impassable. They realise themselves, and serve to shew to others, that there is a gradation of power which leads, little by little, to omnipotence. There is the possibility of getting into perceptual contact with the oversoul which, in its fullest commingling, is what we should conceive as practical omniscience. "The Father and I are one," said the *Christ*. And this because His union with the source of all things was complete. The most highly developed men fall far short of even a remote approach to such magnificence.

But there is promise in the words, *"Be ye therefore perfect even as the Father which is in Heaven is perfect."* The way is indicated. *"Seek ye first the Kingdom."* These are the words of a *mystic*. They must be interpreted mystically. There must be a cultivation of those internally carried powers. There must be an opening of the higher centres of being to the finer pulsations from the spiritual fount of life. The ego, the higher self, must be awakened to the impulses from above and beyond. Then there will be a stirring of the perceptions.

Then, instead of misty notions dimly perceived to bear some little relation to coming events, there will be a fuller, wider knowledge of what is to befall. The distorted suggestiveness of omens will be replaced by a conscious preparation for the future, which will be determined and foreknown by the actions of the present.

CHAPTER VIII

HEALING

PERSONAL AND ABSENT TREATMENT

WESTERN SCIENCE has taught one to regard the body of any living organism as a structure built up from a system of cells or atoms, from the first protoplasmic germ, forming the embryo, to the full-grown creature—animal or human, as may be.

But this physical organism is not all, behind it is the life-giver—*that potent power of spirit*—that *"something"* which makes the chemical substances of which man is formed, a living, breathing entity—that *"something"* which, when withdrawn, leaves but a lump of cold clay.

The man is dead. Blood, bones, sinews, nerves, all are there, only the spirit has fled.

Spirit is the vitalizing substance of the blood, spirit ordains every vibration of the nervous system, spirit is so intermingled with flesh that only advanced psychics can understand truly in what manner, and how this amalgamation takes place.

Spirit is not only the vitalizing substance of the body, but it is also the substance of every thought, so that in the treatment of disease we must consider spirit, and discover in what manner the flow is impeded, and how certain centres of the system are clogged. Remove the cause, permitting the spirit force to resume its normal course, and health again reigns supreme.

Here we have soul and body, the inner vibrations of the spirit aided by outer and protecting vibrations, the outer force which permeates the body having its headquarters at the point where vitality centres.

Every living creature is connected with infinity by the invisible *astral* body, which forms the intermediate link between spirit and matter, and the things which are unseen may be found only through this *astral* body, the spirit of which I speak, so that upon the proper understanding of this may be said to depend the proper grasp of such a wide and extensive theme as *Mental Healing*.

Not only have we to consider bodily ills, but mental conditions which are akin to sickness, and the still larger question of spiritual development and the control of our psychic forces.

Depression, fear, lack of confidence, hopelessness—all these things are diseases, or a *"lack of ease."*

They are mental *states*, due to improper connection between the brain and the vitalizing forces, and they can be removed by an adjustment of those forces by the means best suited to the particular person who is the sufferer.

With some a healing thought will accomplish what is necessary. With others the thought must be further augmented by the spoken word—*suggestion*. Others again need the objective mind to be steeped in unconsciousness, so that appeal may be made to the *subjective* spiritual centre through *Hypnotism*, and yet again, others call for the laying on of hands, or the application of magnetic healing.

But let us have no confusion of thought over these distinctions, for they are all but various phases of *Mental Science*, and they all set out to accomplish the same end—the healing of mind or body without the use of drugs or internal remedies.

Every strong, healthy man and woman possesses a certain amount of natural animal magnetism, it does not consist of good looks or a fine physique, but it does depend upon a correctly maintained balance of psychic force, and this balance depends upon health of mind and body.

When the nerve currents are subjected to outside influences of a disturbing nature they are naturally upset, but they can be easily influenced by a controlled "*Will,*" and the balance re-adjusted.

A strong mentality and a correspondingly strong magnetism can set free the psychic force, and restore the disturbed balance to the magnetic atoms of that body, and so restoring a condition of health where disease reigned previously.

From the above it will be easily seen that by regulating the influences cast upon us, and by recognizing the necessity for *Rest* and short periods of seclusion daily, we can recuperate lost energy, and restore the spiritual life currents to their natural channel.

When this spirit, acting through the astral body, expresses itself through perfect volition in its action upon the organic structure, the body is in a condition of perfect health and harmony, in a condition to ward off every ill state, and especially diseases of a contagious or atmospheric nature, such as influenza or colds.

Few possess this power of volition!

If you take a severe cold you do so when the body is tired, or when you are worried and depressed, never when all the bodily forces are in a state of activity.

When a positive mental condition is lowered the tendency is even more marked than in weariness of the flesh, because the central point has been interrupted, and the whole system thrown into disorder, a prey to any adverse influence which may happen to step in.

This explanation bears out my teachings that— *positive people are seldom ailing.*

The mind is focussed at certain vital centres in the

body, and from them distributes the spiritual force through the body.

If those central points are interrupted, vitality leaves that centre, and disease reigns in its stead.

It is by these means that *mind* quickens, or fails to quicken every globule of blood in the body, and is distributed throughout the entire system.

There is a connecting link, a force which connects the nervous system with the mind, and by controlling this force we keep the body in health.

First, let us consider the influence of *mind* over the inorganic functions of the body.

The actions of a living body (animal or human) may be divided into two—*voluntary and involuntary.*

Roughly speaking, the former may be said to include all action which is the direct result of brain command or desire, such as walking, speaking, eating, moving the body, etc.

The involuntary actions are those of the heart and internal organs, the machinery which works the body, and upon the proper action of which the well-being of the body depends.

It can now be seen clearly that something more than the physical organism has to be taken into account, and that the action of heart, lungs, liver, kidneys, and so forth are dependent upon the free and unimpeded flow of life and vital force to every part of the body, and that this must be taken into consideration when treating anyone for bodily or mental disorders.

It is also a fact that mental conditions cause certain organs of the body to become upset, and in the same way certain organs when disorganized set up a corresponding mental unrest.

Look how miserable bilious people are, how ready to take a jaundiced view of life in general. It would almost seem that "liver" and pessimism were synonymous.

HEALING

Note how sudden fear will affect the action of the heart, and how a "touch of the spleen" is another way of saying a man is in a nasty humor and best left alone!

Anybody who gives way to a violent fit of temper or grief can upset the whole body and divert the life force from nearly every vital centre, proving as disastrous as a thunder-storm to an electric battery. Mean people with a bad temper, have bad health.

In this chapter I will deal with actual facts, to explain the conditions which rule and govern the spiritual, mental and physical amalgamation which we call man, and to make it clear how *thought* and *mind* govern us, and *why*, before I deal with the philosophy or practice of the science.

The life forces collect at certain nerve centres in the body, these are known to physiologists as ganglionic centres, and can be seen in any good work on *Physiology* or *Anatomy*.

They consist chiefly of three great groups or centres, known as the *"cardiac plexus,"* in the region of the heart, the *"solar plexus,"* in the region of the stomach, and the *"sacral plexus,"* in the region of the generative organs.

At the base of the brain we get the principal centre of the body and of Mind.

The *psychic* centre is between the eye-brows, and the principal magnetic centres are the palms of the hands and the eyes.

So we have to consider the different phases of life force categorically.

First.—The blood and its circulation, and the bones, nerves and tissues of the body.

Second.—Human magnetism, which is, briefly, a series of vibrations which tend to the attraction between the vital elements of

122   THE CAVE OF THE ORACLE

   the body and other elements which surround it.
Third.—Nerve force, that which forms a means of transit for spirit or magnetism.
Fourth.—The ethereal body, or psychic aura.
Fifth.—Spirit, the vitalizing element, which permeates all.

The blood and its circulation, etc., we need not consider here.

Human magnetism I have already gone into, and the object of the nerve force is primarily to distribute the *psychic aura*, the atoms of which have to come into contact with the vital centres of the physical organism.

The *psychic atom* consists of three distinct parts.

The *First* is magnetic, the *second* is the ethereal atom or element, the *third* comes into being when these two forces are in harmony and vital, the principle of life, the *spirit,* the living, primordial substance upon which the life and well-being of the entire structure is dependent.

The magnetic and ethereal atom becomes disorganized the moment anything occurs to divert the spirit from its proper action, and in the case of death, of course, they become entirely atrophied.

The blood becomes impoverished when there is an insufficient supply of the vitalizing element, or life force, and in the same way the nervous system suffers when the vital force fails to connect the magnetic and ethereal parts of the atom.

These atoms attain their point of contact with the nerve force or *aura,* at the nerve centres, and impart their vitality to the same.

The magnetic sheath approaches from one direction and the ethereal from another, and all nerve diseases, and in fact nearly all bodily ailments, result from some disturbed action of these atoms, when they are either not vitalized, or when they are not generated and distributed along the nervous system; or in other words, when they accumulate without uniting and distributing the vital properties, and in this case they clog the whole nervous system, and as a natural result derangement of the entire organism sets up.

So the magnetic particle or sheath receives and holds the ethereal particle, which together hold the spiritual and vitalizing substance, thus forming the only connection between body and spirit.

Where these vitalized atoms are found in the body, there also will be found health, energy, and vitality, and where they are absent there will be none, even though the blood circulates and the body is apparently in good condition.

The various methods of restoring the vital flow will be given later, but I think that this will give a clear and concise idea of the cause of disturbance, and *how* it is possible for magnetic and mental stimulus (*applied scientifically*), to readjust these atoms, and to do so more successfully than would be possible through the medium of physic.

I want to prove that there is truth in the old adage, *"Like cures like,"* but I am not urging my readers to condemn or *dispense* entirely with medical men, for although many diseases of a simple nature, due merely to a derangement of the *vital forces,* can be cured by mental treatment, there are other illnesses which most assuredly need medical treatment.

But most of the ills of life, and some of the greater, or so-called *"incurable"* diseases, will often yield to these treatments when medicine has failed entirely to give relief. But even then the quality of faith is very essential if we wish to bring about a real cure. It seems in some way to act upon the psychic atoms of itself, and to readjust them, again showing the power of mind over matter. *"He who wants to obtain true faith must know, because faith grows out of spiritual knowledge."*

A positive mind and a thoroughly cheerful outlook upon life serves to keep disease or trouble at bay, and is as fine a tonic as anyone can buy at the chemist's, finer!

It would appear that any sudden excitement had the effect of readjusting the polarization of the magnetic and psychic atom, and so allowing the vital force freedom of movement.

This is not theory, but a fact borne out by countless millions of cases one reads about and hears of every day.

This explanation then gives a *reason* for the effects obtained by *Mental Science,* and it also gives a reason why the science fails in some cases and in others succeeds for a time, only to drop into uselessness.

I shall be looked upon as a fearful heretic by Mental Scientists in general, I fear, for even suggesting that the science could fail, but I am *not writing for them,* but for those people who want the truth, and because I want to see it firmly placed upon a common-sense basis, where it can be really useful to all

ABSENT TREATMENT

The application of mind or *Spiritual Healing* is one of the most useful, and at the same time most abused forms of the *Occult sciences.*

I would have it distinctly understood that mind, under certain conditions can, and does, effect wonderful cures.

The chief essential in what is technically known as *absent* treatment is passivity on the part of the patient.

It naturally is of great assistance if the patient being cognizant of treatment, has faith in the healer's power to bring him ease, and to disperse the evil conditions which surround him.

HEALING

But it is not *necessary*.

The patient in some cases may be quite ignorant of the fact that treatment is being administered.

Passivity is the essential point. A patient who is actively antagonistic to the treatment will not get the best help.

Before going into the conditions attached to the patient, however, I will deal with the necessary attitude and work of the *Healer*.

Nobody who lacks power of concentration, and a good share of that elusive quality called *magnetism*, should dream of taking up *Mental Healing* at all.

To begin with we must consider what is the primary cause of disease; this I have already explained fully on the previous pages, and it is readily understood that if one person's *Healing Force* is to act upon the diseased body of another, that person must be mentally stronger and more organized than the one who is to be treated.

A thought to have any carrying power must be like a clearly-cut cameo, a complete mental picture. If you will take note of the conditions under which telepathic messages are received clearly by people who are *not experimenting* in the matter, you will find it is invariably under the strain of some intense emotion, when every faculty of the person who sends the message is strained, often to breaking point, upon the subject in hand.

Few people have this habit of visualization, for most are far too lazy to take the trouble to acquire it.

It entails the habit of close observation and attention, the lack of which is the cause of most cases of bad memory.

The *Healer* cannot possibly expect any results if he cannot send a healing force to the patient.

To heal mentally you must ignore the diseased condition of the patient, and replace that image with one of perfect health.

All *Mental Healing* is due to the projection of healing forces and suggestion. In absent healing it is suggested by telepathy, so that the desired condition is suggested or affirmed by the *Healer,* and all adverse conditions are to be put on one side and ignored entirely.

Each treatment should last from forty minutes to an hour, and the *Healer* will find it best to keep regular times for treatment, repeating it twice daily, which is enough for most cases.

Presuming the patient is agreeable and cognizant of the treatment, it will always create more impression if a clearly typed or written page of instructions is sent to him.

Your whole endeavor is to impress.

Let the patient lie or recline in an easy chair at the given time. Every muscle should be relaxed, and perfect ease and comfort studied. It is not enough to secure bodily relaxation however, the mind must also relax, and a passive, more or less sleepy condition is the best to be assumed.

Banish all care or thought of ill or worry, do not trouble over anything material, but just feel that strong and radiant life forces are being infused into the pain-weary body, and that health will reign in place of disease.

This is by no means so easy to do as it would appear, but the great thing essential to successful treatment is to have the patient in a thoroughly receptive and passive condition. *He may even sleep if he likes, it will not interfere with the treatment at all.*

Then, yourself, sit in a comfortable chair, for ease of body produces ease of mind, and call up a mental vision of your patient. If it is somebody you have never seen you should procure a photograph, for it is not easy to treat somebody of whose very personality you are ignorant.

HEALING

I may state here, in parenthesis, that it is always best to treat yourself *first* of all, and then steadfastly affirm your ability to heal the sick person.

Calling him by name, your treatment may proceed much as follows:—

"So and so, I hold you in the Infinite Good, perfect health is yours, your mind and body are at ease, and ALL *is well with you. You are well, you are strong, you are full of radiant health, and all is harmony within you. You are full of life force, of the Divine Being, health and ease dominate you. Health reigns within you, you are well, you are perfect, radiant life."*

You will find this short and simple *formula* sufficient, and you repeat with growing intensity until you can call up your patient before you as it were in life, and insist upon the condition of health he enjoys.

As you contemplate the mental vision you see a stream of healing magnetism passing from your brain to his body, enveloping it, bathing it, soothing and healing, until all the living tissues spring into action, and, thus stimulated by the magnetism of your healing force, fall to work to complete the work you have begun.

To many it is incredible how anybody can be healed at a distance like this, but the fact remains, *it can be done, and it is done.*

Thought is a more powerful agent than many are willing to admit, but not everybody's thought.

It must be *concentrated, intense, powerful,* or it will miss the mark and nothing will result.

But beyond all else that habit of visualization is *most* important, a blurred image can bring no definite result, there must be a clear conception of every *detail,* form, color, clothes, expression and so forth, unless this is obtained nothing will happen.

You must not recognize the disease in your patient, and you must have perfect faith in your *ability to heal,* through health currents, with your mind. *Mental Healing*, especially when absent, is the most difficult form of suggestion.

So much depends upon the power of concentration, for without this thought, or suggestion on the wings of thought, cannot travel.

All is vibration, and it is, in the case of healing like this, sympathetic thought vibration traveling through the cosmic force and arousing the slumbering vibratory forces in the sick man.

We cannot say that sickness is *not*, that all is well with him, but we choose to IGNORE the evil condition for our own purpose and in order to arouse the dormant forces to action.

Success does not always come, nor does success come at once like the touch of a magic wand, although I have known cases where the improvement was almost magical, if not quite so.

The *Healer* must be free from adverse thought images, and must himself be steeped, *literally*, with the impression of health, or he cannot impress it upon others.

Bear in mind that you are treating the SUBJECTIVE man, not the objective, it is the ego you are dealing with rather than the body.

To obtain a given effect it is often better to *exaggerate* than to under-act your part, so that you carry your own conception almost to the point of ecstasy.

It is not wise to attempt the sole treatment of dangerous cases where life is in danger. The healer may aid the physician, and very powerfully so, but I do not consider that Mental Healing has reached that stage of perfection where drugs and doctors can be dispensed with at a crisis.

But there are hundreds of cases where it can be used effectively and alone.

In colds, coughs, rheumatism, constipation, gout, and

HEALING

a host of diseases that whilst not serious are very obstinate, and *do not yield* so easily to drugs as to mind power and suggestion.

I have on one occasion cured a woman who was given up by the doctors at the birth of her child, and in a fortnight she was quite well, although no hope had been held out for her recovery.

But in dealing with the former diseases I think it is best to let the patient co-operate.

It is no use treating a person for constipation if they continue to lead a sedentary existence with no exercise, and eating improper diet. Yet constipation, which is at the root of almost every trouble the body is heir to, is easily cured by mental treatment, although I certainly advocate regular exercise and suitable diet.

Brown bread, green meat, oranges and so forth, whilst half a pound of Brazil nuts daily are excellent.

In healing a case of constipation I always make a very vivid mental picture of the patient's bowels, and see them in a perfectly liquid condition. Not a very pleasant treatment possibly, but when properly done wonderfully effective.

In curing liver complaints also I generally attack the bowels also, and place special concentrated thought upon the liver, gall bladder and so forth.

From this it will be seen that in curing any specific disease it is as well to place special thought currents at the centre of disturbance, but always taking care not to recognize the diseased conditions, but rather to emphasize and to *exaggerate* the condition of health, as in the case of constipation, the exaggerated treatment of the bowels acting like an aperient and clearing all the refuse away.

Ease of mind and ease of body are essential to the successful healer, and without them little can be done.

Any sudden emotion will frequently dispel pain, but very often the only emotion present is the consciousness of being on the rack, and with this dominant the healing forces cannot, as is easily understood, work with the necessary freedom. It is a pitched battle, and as a rule pain wins.

On the other hand, the set determination to carry on one's work in spite of sickness or pain will very often result in dispelling the pain, and enable one to *"keep on going,"* where other folk would be in bed with a doctor and a *"temperature."*

I've done it very often myself with no ill results, but I don't advise others to do it, not on my recommendation at any rate, for it is a well-known maxim that *"one man may steal a horse whilst another may not look over the stable door,"* and whilst I possess the constitution of a trained Adept and Master of the occult, others not so blessed might suffer severely for what I can do with impunity.

But at the same time I hold that will is paramount when the pain is not too bad to let it dominate and work its way for the freedom of the forces.

HOW TO GIVE A TREATMENT

THIS is one of the most interesting phases of *Healing* and is in reality what is known as *"Magnetic or Mental Healing."* I will also give here further instructions for Magnetic Healing proper.

I may state at the outset that not everybody is *qualified* for this work. Such people must be not only *spiritually* filled, but must also possess the requisite magnetism for the purpose.

Sufficient magnetism may be to a certain extent acquired for every-day use, say, but I do not think a thoroughly negative person with hardly any magnetism can obtain a supply strong enough to effect a cure of any disease.

Those with a knowledge of *Palmistry* can easily judge, for when the Mount of the *Moon* encroaches

HEALING

upon the Mount of *Mars* (over the Mercury Mount) on the percussion of the hand, forming a lump or mount of its own, then you may be sure that person possesses a plentiful supply, and only needs teaching *how* to use it.

Before treatment is undertaken the student must become familiar with the various magnetic and electric centres of the body.

I will enumerate and classify them clearly:—
1.—Psychic centre, between the brows.
2.—The principal centre or "pole" of the body, at the base of the brain.
3.—The bronchial centre, or the throat (front).
4.—Pulmonary centre, the upper chest and lungs.
5.—The lower lungs and cardiac centre—centre seated above the heart.
6.—The centre for stomach, liver, and digestive organs, seated just above the navel.
7.—Vital and generative centres, at the base of stomach.
8.—Principal magnetic centres, or the palms of the hands.
9.—Electric centres, the soles of the feet (seldom used).

Operations always start from "1," when treating a patient.

It is of course clearly understood that the healer must be in perfect health, and complete master of his own will power.

For treatment the healer should first induce his own magnetic flow by briskly rubbing the hands together, and tensing the muscles of hand and arm, then relaxing. Do this three or four times, opening and shutting the hand as the muscles relax and contract.

Now place your right hand at the base of the patient's brain as described above, holding it for five minutes to allow the magnetic current from your hand to pass through the entire system. As I have already pointed out, there is a special centre for each organ, but this one at the base of the brain is headquarters.

In treatment connection is first set up with headquarters, then with the centre governing the organ which is out of order, and *not,* be it noted, with the organ itself.

The hand which is used in healing is the principal magnetic pole of the body, and when holding it to the base of operation the muscles should be *tensed,* and a very slight quivering movement given to the hand, this I may say will follow naturally on the tensed muscles.

In a healthy person the hand is capable of discharging strong magnetic currents, and the healer, by applying his hand to the centres of another person, sends this current right through the body, for at these centres only can such a charge of magnetism enter, and having entered proceed to vivify the entire system.

Man, in common with most things in nature, generates an *aura,* that is to say a mist-like envelope emanates from his body, invisible to the physical eye, which assumes different forms and colors according to the spiritual, mental and physical condition of the man.

But there is also another *aura* known as the health *aura,* or nerve *aura,* which is connected with health conditions only, it is generated by the nervous system and is entirely or almost entirely under the influence of spirit, and when any derangements are set up in the system it is through this nerve *aura* and the nervous system generally that the magnetic forces reach the various organs of the body.

The organs do not become diseased of themselves, but only through a stoppage in the life supply which is carried to them by the nervous system, and the moment the full supply of spirit or life force is inter-

HEALING

cepted that moment diseased conditions are set up, the irritation gradually increasing, often affecting the whole system and remaining until the stoppage is cleared.

The magnetic and other forces which not only exist in the blood (as I have described elsewhere), but are to be found freely in the *aura* surrounding every living object, are very sensitive to conditions and emanations from other bodies and are apt to take these up freely and convey them through the entire organism, especially when the person chances to be tired, unwell, or in a negative, non-resisting condition.

This condition is peculiarly frequent in people leading sedentary lives, for they not only feel tired, but their muscles are flabby from want of use, the blood is frequently over-heated from an improper or too liberal diet, and they catch every disease afloat, from a cold to measles, or worse.

That is one reason why I so strongly recommend physical culture, because when the muscles are developed, the whole body fit and braced up, the man or woman is naturally in a positive condition and will seldom attract disease or other undesirable conditions, which as a rule only fasten upon the negative or weakly.

By contact with the body the healer immediately sets up sympathetic action in the nerve aura of the patient, and by the positive and magnetic power of his own aura stimulates the disordered cells and awakens them to action.

In cases of extreme weakness, I do not advise more than a two minutes' contact, for sometimes in these cases the patient is unable to stand the sudden flow of vitality.

You can accomplish nothing if you do not use your will power and concentrate your attention upon the patient and the flow of vitality which you wish to pass through to the patient, for without concentration and attention the flow will only pass through imperfectly, and sometimes not at all.

With *very* weak or sensitive persons contact need not take place at all, and the magnetic current may be projected through the centres by will power alone.

However, having by contact (or otherwise) established *rapport* with the patient, remove the hands from both the base of the brain and also that centre which answers to the diseased parts of the body, then, with still tensed muscles, and strongly willing the magnetic flow from your fingers and hands make circular passes, starting at the base of the brain, next over the seat of disease, then to include the entire system.

These passes begin in a small circle, not touching the body, but at a distance of about three inches away, the sweep of the circle increasing as the other centres of the body are gradually taken into the treatment.

Occasionally you may touch the hands of your patient, and in very rare instances the feet, but do not ever do this last mentioned unless the patient is strong enough to bear it.

There are two distinct types of patient who will come under your control, those who are known as *magnetic*, and those who are called *electric* in temperament.

Magnetic people are dark, and as a rule pale (I am not referring here to the quality of animal magnetism which is often possessed alike by both types), and generally liverish; electric people are fair, and as a rule nervous and retiring in nature.

The extremely magnetic temperament is rarely sensitive, the extremely electric temperament is usually so to a very high degree.

Between these two lie all the various temperaments that go to make up mankind.

In treating the electric temperament make these cir-

HEALING

cular passes in a *downward* direction, from the brain to the heart.

In treating the *magnetic* temperament reverse the order of things, the passes should be made in an upward direction, with the object of stimulating the brain centres.

The treatments should vary in time according to the condition of the patient, and as I have explained different passes must be used for the magnetic or electric temperament.

In the case of bronchitis, colds, coughs, etc., it is best to first treat the entire system, commencing at the base of the brain, making the passes in circular direction from the front of the throat, gradually increasing the circles to take in the centres of the lungs, heart, stomach and digestive organs, all of which need stimulating to a greater state of activity.

The palms of the hands may be treated by contact for one minute, and the treatment finished by applying your hand at the base of the brain, or centre 2.

Never place your hand on the top of a patient's head.

Repeat treatment two or three times a day in severe cases, but once a day, for twenty minutes, is sufficient for ordinary cases.

It is always best to have the patient in a warm room and clad in a very light wrapper during treatment.

In treating cases of heart disease or palpitation great care is necessary, on no account must the healer touch magnetic or electric centres, *i.e.*, the palms of the hands or the soles of the feet.

Send the magnetic vibrations from the base of the brain, then make the circular passes close to the body from in front, over the heart centre, to include the pulmonary centre. Treat daily.

In consumption much benefit can be obtained by a persistent following out of this treatment. Make the passes back and front, first establishing contact as before described, then, after treating the centres for the lungs, go over the other centres of the body, sending a slight shock of about two minutes' duration through the palms of the hands.

Treat daily, let the patient live as much as possible out of doors, and eat plenty of plain but nourishing food.

In the treatment of biliousness and liver, and kindred complaints, troubles which usually attack magnetic people, the whole system needs rousing.

Let the patient take a cold bath, of one minute's duration, night and morning.

Treat the centres of heart and liver, and also of the stomach and digestive organs, the former back and front, the latter from the front only.

Contact through the soles of the feet may be established, for one minute only, in these cases. Place your hand firmly against the naked feet, sending a strong current right through the body.

Sick headache will take the same treatment as the above. It is a question of stomach and not head!

In rheumatism the whole body should be treated, and the centres eight and nine, magnetic and electric also.

In cases of rheumatism of the lower limbs, the hands, strongly charged with magnetism, may be passed along the legs from thigh to ankle, and contact with the electric centres be established for *two* minutes.

A liberal and regular diet of celery will do much to rout rheumatism, even in chronic cases.

For treatment of toothache, neuralgia, and similar ailments, the whole body requires treatment, and the warm hand of the healer may be applied temporarily to the seat of pain, passes being made from thence to the base of the brain.

To cure mumps make the circular passes over the bronchial centres, but from the back of the body, and finish up with a general treatment.

For lumbago the treatment consists of treating first the centres of the brain, then establish contact at the bottom of the spine, and treat further by circular passes over the back of the body, over centre 6, the vital centres, etc.

For hysteria treat the whole body in a series of circular passes, remembering *not to touch the palms of the hands or soles of feet,* hysterical people are generally electric and highly nervous.

Influenza will usually yield to treatment administered over the poles of the pulmonary centres, and from the magnetic centres, palms of hands.

Treatment should be given three or four times daily, and will soon show results if properly administered.

For eczema and skin diseases generally first treat the entire body, then move the hands in circular passes very close to, but not touching the body, let the patient drink magnetized water, and also bathe the affected part with some.

To magnetize the water make passes over it in a shallow vessel, strongly tensing the muscles of the arms as you do so.

Great relief will be given almost immediately in the case of asthma, by treating the bronchial and pulmonary centres, from back to front, with magnetic contact of two or three minutes with the hands, or magnetic centres of the patient.

The general treatment, if persisted in, will act as a sleeping draught, and cure even the worst cases of insomnia, probably in a period of two, or at the outside, three weeks.

In the treatment of sciatica commence with contact at the base of the brain and the end of the spinal column, followed by five minutes' contact with the electric centres (soles of feet) and circular passes from the base of the brain to the centre marked "7" at the beginning of this chapter.

As the success of the treatment depends to a great extent upon a certain nervous sympathy between the patient and healer, it is best not to attempt treatment of such cases where this sympathy does not exist.

Remember that your vibrations are positive, and that you must regulate the length of contact and closeness of the passes by the condition of your patient, for in cases of extreme weakness your vigorous magnetism may prove more than the patient can bear.

Allow your invisible helpers in the spirit world to guide you as to length of treatment, etc., and avoid treating those temperaments which clash with your own, for you will only harm them.

Above all, always remember the difference in the passes for magnetic and electric patients, electric in downward circles, magnetic upwards.

"Self-Healing" is not possible by these means, as can be readily understood.

CHAPTER IX

MENTAL TELEPATHY

IN a previous chapter reference was made to the *etheric* senses of man. Impressions were said to be obtained with them by the *psychometrist*, and brought over to the physical plane as sensations. It will be well, perhaps, here to review briefly the ground already covered. In *alchemy* the universality and homogeneity of substance were traced. Mother earth, the basis of our own physical form, it was demonstrated, was in essence differing modes of expression of the underlying substance, ether. In *Astrology*, the gravitational and other physical influences of the celestial bodies were correlated to their *electrical* influences. From this it was inferred that there would also be mental or psychic influences. In *psychometry*, the argument is carried further. The *etheric* substratum of the globe and the *etheric* substratum of man were shown to be mutually affectable and affected. The so-called inorganic matter of science was held to be impressible by the psychic emanations of man. Such impressions were reconvertible. Now we have to deal with the capacity of man to communicate with man by these same *etheric* senses and organs. For telepathy is the power of communication of mind to mind without the intervention of the normal channels of correspondence of physical sense impressions, sight and sound.

Years ago there was a vogue of so-called *thought-reading*. Physical contact was made between operator and subject and a hidden article was located, the operator being guided to the spot by the subject. Various theories were elaborated to account for the success which attended these exhibitions. The usually accepted conclusion was that involuntary muscular action, induced by nerve strain in the subject, indicated to the operator sufficiently clearly the way to go. The nerve strain was, of course, induced by the subject concentrating his thoughts on the object. This *thought-reading* so-called was, however, of the earth earthy. For it simply substituted for the normal modes, sight and sound, another physical sense, touch. In *Telepathy* we have to deal with the possibility of conveyance of impressions in situations where the use of sight and sound and touch would be equally superseded, if not actually impossible, by reason of the limitations of space. It is evident that direct transmission of thought could transcend spatial limits. *For thought is not subject to our physical three-dimensionized plane.* It is no more difficult to carry the thought to the further side of the world than to the further side of the room. Indeed, the infinite capacity of the universe is the only limitation of thought, if it has any limits at all.

It will be necessary, in the first place, in analyzing a specific instance of *Telepathy*, to make fully plain the meanings of the terms now to be employed. I will define precisely the meaning to be conveyed by the term *"mind,"* and then consider the functions of the mind, and the *"faculties"* employed in so functioning. The ordinary dictionary definition will serve our purpose for *"mind,"* which is given alternately as *"the understanding,"* or *"the whole spiritual nature of man."* By this is clearly implied that part of a man's nature which is not *"material."* Leaving out of the question the philosophical aspect of immortality or permanence, we will agree to call the *"mind"* that portion of the man which is not subject to the limitations of our three-dimensionized space. It is that within the man which enables him to *"think,"* to *"plan,"* to *"will,"* to *"imagine."* Whether thought be a function of "matter," as some materialists have it, or not, does not really affect the issue. Thought is a *"function,"* the doing of something, and the doing of something is clearly the exercise of *"force."*

Any cause which changes, or tends to change, a body's state of rest or motion, is a force. And whether we think of thought as causing the movement in the brain cells, or of undulations in the ether, as light and electricity do, it is still a force with which we are dealing. *The "will" is the supreme faculty of the mind.* Thought and imagination its two principal functions. Thought, again, being a force, has the capacity to do work, and the work will produce in its turn an equivalent amount of energy of another form. In thinking the simplest form of energy exhibited is that shown as chemical energy in *"cerebration,"* dissociation or aggregation, of the physical particles of the brain cells. The energy which is produced by the work done, in this building up, or breaking down process, is given out again as etheric undulations. These, like light, are invisible or inaudible till reflected or refracted. Light itself is an invisible undulation, in an invisible medium. This is proved thus. A beam of light projected into a darkened chamber becomes visible only by the *"reflection"* from the surfaces of the tiny particles which float in the air. If these particles —in any portion of the path of the beam—be consumed, by the application of a bunsen burner, which has no light flame, a distinct track of *"invisible light"* will be presented, as darkness. The *"thought-undulations"* of the ether require, then, a substance capable of reflecting or refracting them to make them become visible or audible. The alternative is used advisedly, because we know that it is possible for energy of one sort to change into energy of another kind or form. Light, heat and sound are but differences in pitch of vibration rate.

We now instance a case in *Telepathy*. A quotation of *Shakespeare* is to be transmitted. As the transmitter reads the passage his *"thought"* is consciously or unconsciously at work. To read the passage he must first exercise his will to perceive it, his thought to apprehend, his memory to record it. He cannot himself apprehend what is written without *"thinking."* The act of thinking causes the brain cells to move (even materialists admit this), and by their action a new form of energy is produced—etheric undulations. These undulations, like those of light, spread in all directions with inconceivable rapidity. They impress all bodies within their range with a *"latent image"* which can be evoked by *psychometry*. But they do more. They impress also the brain cells with a *"stress"* which may or may not be appreciable. If the brain impressed be *"sensitized,"* by conscious preparation of cell-structure (polarized by thought-energy), the immediate transformation of the *"stress"* is manifested by etheric undulations appreciable by the mind of the *"subject,"* as vividly, as accurately, and as immediately as are the thoughts of his own volition. And, at the séance, what of the brain cells of the audience? is the cry of the sceptic. Why do they not respond to the *"stress"*? Practically because in their case there is no developer to render the latent image perceptible.

In *Hypnotism,* when a subject is put into the trance condition, and a suggestion, post-dated so to speak, is given, the subject when aroused will be unconscious of the suggestion itself, or of the time when it is to take effect. That such really occurs there can be no doubt, as the accuracy of the fact has been repeatedly proved. In this case we see an instance of a mind, impressing itself as a thought or command, as *"stress"* upon the brain cells of another, to act in a certain manner at a certain time. Yet when the sleep is terminated, the subject of it knows nothing. When the time approaches to act, he will, however, act, as if of his own volition, in the manner suggested by the operator. The thought *"impressed"* has created a stress which, when suitable conditions are provided, will liberate the energy to complete the action. During the *hypnosis*—induced sleep, it will be noted—the normal functioning of the mind of the subject is inhibited, inactive. The operator imposes his will by thought-suggestion, as the *"force"* to do. But on recovery no trace of this *"imposition"* is apparent. It is latent, however, and emerges into actuality later only, when conditions permit the energy, present as a "passive stress," to transform.

In like manner with those present at a séance. The stress is, virtually, imposed upon all equally, by the thoughts of the operator, but it is prevented from reacting by the normal functioning of the other faculties. Suitable conditions would evoke it, as the *"latent image,"* from an indifferently sensitized plate, confused and blurred, and possibly utterly unrecognizable. In the other case we have instanced there is, instead, a "new plate," freshly *"sensitized"* for each *"impression."* And this is developed, fixed and printed, instantaneously, to use the more familiar photographic analogy.

This power of *Telepathy* is one which all of the human race possess *in potentio,* but not developed yet for actual use. In the case of some people constant effort has brightened and polished the faculty to such an extent that it is as *"normal"* to them as speech is now to the remainder of the species.

Surprising as the last statements may appear, they can easily be demonstrated by simple experiments. To some it will appear so easy to acquire a slight command of this *"power"* that the only wonderful thing about it will then be that they were not conscious of their ability before. To others, who will make the same experiments without the slightest vestige of success, the proofs must lie in the reasonableness and consistency of the hypothesis. It has been said that this faculty is latent in the vast majority. Its development will depend upon the amount of use to which it is put. On the physical plane we do not expect the *"athlete"* to develop in a starved and stunted frame; especially if no effort is made to train. So with the mind and its powers. Will, its supreme faculty, rarely receives conscious training to render it *"fit."* Thought, the chief function of the mind, is also rarely *"exercised,"* and consciously directed, as it should be. Most people just *"drift"* instead of thinking.

The ancient philosophers held that if the will were concentrated with persistence, the subject of its thought might, in time, be made to take objective reality. This is, in effect, what *telepathists* do, to a lesser degree. The *"thoughts,"* consciously impelled, actually take objective reality, visibly or audibly, to the recipient's more finely strung inner senses. It is in this "conscious" direction of the thoughts, and a specially attuned *"condition"* to receive and reproduce them, that the apparent mystery of *Telepathy* is contained. But in it there is nothing incompatible with the teachings of modern science.

For the more or less perfect transmission of thought, two conditions are imperative. There must be a conscious effort to transmit and a conscious effort to receive. I leave for the moment as a side issue the phenomena of *Hypnotism,* for I have fully dealt with this subject in my books which teach Hypnotism and *Mesmerism.* Instances are constantly recurring, which cannot be explained by coincidence, of unconscious transmission of thought. Two persons in the same room will be affected by the same train of thought, or it may be the same refrain of a melody, and when one gives audible utterance to it, the other will remark, "*How strange!* That has been running through my brain." One person will hesitate in speaking for a word that will not come, or in writing for a similar cause. The bystander will think of the word, but possibly before he utters it, the other has also caught the unconsciously projected etheric vibration. This provides an opportunity for exercise. If one be of active mental disposition it is not difficult always to provide the word. And the test may be made more certain by the transmission of an unsuitable word which will be accepted immediately and unhesitatingly, and then rejected when reflection has shown its unsuitability. Such instances are, however, only the first childlike stumbling from the *"all fours"* position to the erect and down again.

When one has mastered the will sufficiently to concentrate the thought, and consciously to project it, a helping hand may be held out to the recipient whose task is somewhat more difficult. For here the mind has to be rendered blank. The plate has to be sensitized, but excluded from the ordinary light rays. Only to those which pass through the lens must it respond. The condition of mental passivity is an extremely difficult one to attain. Much of what passes for thinking is mere drifting. And the very effort of trying not to think carries the untrained mind instantly into shoal water. Yet we can teach ourselves not to think. The mind can be rendered passive to a greater or lesser degree. The mind controls the body always to some extent. The emotions sway and distort the physical frame. Fear, anger and joy will induce complex physical changes in the nervous, muscular, bony and tissue structures of the body. But the emotions can be controlled by the will. The will exerted consciously and constantly and powerfully will make a man almost insusceptible to emotional stresses. Man's mental principle acting through his etheric body can attain almost complete mastery over the physical body.

It is then that the possibility of telepathy becomes apparent as a normal function. The thought transmitted by another awakens the etheric sense of the recipient as the wave oscillation of the marconigram actuates the coherer. The local circuit is closed and the message is materialized in the relay. There is nothing mysterious about it, though to the uninitiated the transmission of *aerial* telepathy is marvelous. But then, so is the more normal mode of telegraphy to those unacquainted with the elements of electrical science. Telephony itself is even more marvelous. For here we have the dissociating of sound-waves, the conversion of mechanical energy into electrical energy, and its conversion into mechanical energy again. In telepathy there is a similar process. The thought energy becomes cerebration or mechanical energy which gives off electrical energy, etheric undulations, these in turn becoming reconverted into mechanical energy or brain movements in the physical body of the recipient, after having been assimilated, as etheric disturbance, by his astral or etheric sense organs.

Of unconscious transmission of thought there are numberless instances on record. Many of them, it will be noted, occur at the time of grave peril or at the point of death. This is suggestive. At such moments the physical body is almost wholly dormant. The consciousness is being exercised on the etheric or even on the mental plane. The recipients, too, are usually those of highly nervous temperament or of imaginative disposition. This is sometimes used as though it were an argument against the validity of such phenomena. The imagination is confused with fancy, as though the two were identical, instead of being, as they are, as wide asunder as the poles. The imaginative individual lives and acts very much on the higher planes of consciousness. In those higher planes the etheric senses are the vehicle. Susceptibility to etheric disturbances is its distinguishing mark. And the unconscious thought-waves impinge upon and impress such individuals because their consciousness is super-normal.

In *Hypnotism* there is a reversal of these conditions. The subject is insensitive to his own etheric disturbances. His physical body is directly controlled by the operator superseding the subject volition. The passivity of the subject and its obedience to external control carries with it its own incapacity to register what occurs. There has been a forcible ejection of the rightful tenant who cannot be expected to be cognizant of the usurper's actions. As a matter of fact, the subject is cognizant because his own etheric vehicle is necessarily used to affect the physical changes.

But a *Hypnotic* subject usually possesses little power of transmission of consciousness from one plane to the other. That his higher principles—his subconscious memory, to use the phrases of *exact* science —do carry over the knowledge of events is proved by the fact that post-suggestion is acted upon. The subject finds it difficult, however, to explain why he does certain things. He merely feels that he must. A triumphant vindication this of the truth of telepathy. The memorized mental suggestion of the operator is obeyed. And it is obeyed by a recipient who has no knowledge, in his normal consciousness, of such a command having been received.

By suggestion, a habitual drunkard, suffering from a veritable fever disease, his whole cellular system polarized by the continued action of the overstimulation of his vibration rate, may be cured. The almost irresistible craving, ever present when in his normal state, to continue the acceleration, is arrested by the thought of the operator, who dominates the system of the subject and compels it to vibrate to its normal rate again. The operator reacts upon the disturbed vibratory system by a process akin to depolarization, and restores harmony and health.

As a matter of fact, the modern physician owes much of his success, in his conflict with both mental and physical disorders, to the exercise, consciously or unconsciously, of his thought-suggestion. The patient *"feels"* that the doctor has the ability to do him good, and the cheerful self-assertiveness of the physician itself is the most powerful assistant he could desire to evoke to aid his drugs.

These, ordinarily, effect their purpose by a stimulation of the organs concerned, in a physical manner; order resulting from chaos by the expenditure of chemical energy. As, however, there is no appreciable difference between the anæsthesia produced by the thought-suggestion, and by a drug, both causing a similar effect by a mode differing in phase, so also there is no difference in the cure of the drunkard. In the one case the mental energy of the thought-suggestion, and in the other the chemical energy of the drugs, has been responsible for the effect. In the case of the hypnotic anæsthesia the action is palpably through the etheric double. Its intimate relationship with the physical compels the latter to respond, immediately, to its own vibration rate.

Materia medica has its limitations, and so doubtless has *Hypnotism*. An infusion of senna, or tincture of iron (both valuable remedies when correctly employed) would not assist very materially in restoring an amputated limb. Nor would *hypnotic* suggestion. But it is a logical conclusion, if the premises be admitted, that minor pathological effects, as distinct from those of a surgical character, can be produced or modified, by *hypnotic* suggestion, in precisely the same manner as would occur if drugs were used instead.

Both the patient and the healer in the practice of

Christian Science exhibit an earnest belief in the possibility of being healed, and healing. This is a condition favorable to the concentraton of effort so necessary for successful *hypnotic* treatment. The prayers of the patient induce a condition of passivity or subjectivity, on his part, and the will of the healer is consciously exerted by his own prayers, which practically assume the form of a command, or suggestion. Given ideal conditions, it would appear quite feasible that a case of scarlet fever could be successfully treated in this way. A reduction of temperature could certainly be ensured by suggestion, and, with a modification of diet, the progress of the disease germs subdued, if not actually arrested, immediately, by a further exhibition of *hypnotic* suggestion. It should be remembered that the disease germs themselves, in common with all other forms of organised life, are resolvable ultimately by introspective analysis into "corpuscular groupings," vibrating with inconceivable rapidity, and amenable to change of rate or grouping by the imposition of differing forces, of which thought energy is one example.

From this brief reference to the phenomena of *hypnotism,* it will be seen that the active transmission of thought, by a conscious operator, is quite a commonplace. Its reception, too, by the sub-conscious mind, and the physical activity resulting from the latter's receptivity, also calls for little comment. It is when the transmitted thought has to be retranslated, as it were, into ideation that we approach once more the occult art of telepathy. The examples given earlier in this chapter indicate plainly a method of empirical research open to all. Passivity can be cultivated. And soon it is comparatively easy to obtain first-hand evidence that telepathy is no more mysterious or wonderful than writing or speaking. It depends upon vibrations of higher pitch than sound—on those approaching to light waves and electrical waves in frequency.

CHAPTER X

CLAIRVOYANCE

In telepathy we carried our argument a stage further than it had previously been advanced. The endeavour was made to substantiate the possibility of the communication of the mind of one individual with another. This was held to be possible by the operation of the etheric sense organs. In *Clairvoyance* we have to deal with the extension of the use of these same etheric senses. For *Clairvoyance* is the power of seeing things outside the range of normal vision. It is proposed to show that the etheric vision is capable of transcending our three-dimensional space.

Now it is first desirable to review the mode of normal vision. We can thus see how far in accord with similar ascertained scientific laws the claims of the *Clairvoyant* may be. Normal vision depends upon the fact that rays of light, which are undulations of the ether, are reflected from the substances upon which they fall. Such rays reflected into space again are focussed by the eye on which, in common with other objects in their path, they strike. The optic nerve is stimulated and the impressions of such stimulus are conveyed to the brain. The etheric undulations are here transformed into vision. That is—we see. How precisely the transformation is effected, from the physical reflex into a mental impression, we do not know. But it is suggested that the etheric double, the astral counterpart of the man, is the medium by which the motion of undulation is converted, or transformed, into and on to a higher plane of consciousness.

Such rays of light as are perceptible to the normal vision, or rather which are capable of stimulating the optic nerve, are only a small section of the almost infinite range of light rays. The eye responds only to the rays of the spectrum. But, above and below it, varying immensely in pitch, or wave-length, and frequency, are others. This is demonstrated by photography and radiography. Heat is molecular motion, light is etheric motion. Electricity is inter-etheric motion. Just as there are sounds too low in pitch and too high in pitch for our normal organs to respond to, so there are etheric vibrations to which our ordinary organs will not, or cannot, respond. But because our ordinary organs fail to identify, or to react to, these vibrations, we are not entitled to say that they do not exist. The same holds with our fundamental notions of weight, of mass, and of opacity and transparency.

Light rays do not penetrate sheets of lead. Light rays do penetrate sheets of glass. This appears commonplace until we examine the statements seriously. Then we find that some light rays do penetrate sheets of lead; and that sheets of glass are quite opaque to the same rays. The ultra violet rays, or X-rays, are referred to. It is seen, therefore, that if there are light rays which behave in this apparently contradictory and extraordinary manner, there is at least a case for inquiry to be made out for *Clairvoyance*, which claims that things can be seen with other means than that of the ordinary light rays, or by means of the ordinary eyes.

It has usually been the custom, in speaking of *Clairvoyance*, to allude to it as *"an alleged power of inner sight."* Some psychologists, students of the mental sciences, might tender the familiar phrase "imagination," forgetting that labelling a thing afresh is by no means equivalent to an intelligent explanation of the phenomenon itself, its cause, or the method of its working. Accepting, for the moment, that *Clairvoyance* may be but the result of the exercise of the function of "imagination," we will endeavour to see how far this would justify the claim made for ability to see things not visibly present to the normal senses.

In a previous chapter, *Telepathy,* allusion was made to the mind of man and its faculties and functions. Taking a stand upon the thesis there laid down, "imagination" is postulated as a function of the mind. The etymology of the word is suggestive and instructive. In its older form, its meaning was *"to contrive," "to devise":* the exercise clearly of a power of *"creation,"* or formation. Imagination, then, is a "force" by virtue of its power to do work, even if that work be nothing more than the production of *"etheric vibrations"* which result from conscious or unconscious "cerebration."

The imagination has often been confused with thought. In reality they are as closely allied as are the positive and negative phases of electricity. As, however, we can treat of the energy of electricity either from its positive side or from its negative side, so also we can view the positive and negative aspects of the mind's energy as manifested in *"thought"* or *"imagination."* Thought is *"positive."* That is, it is so with those who think consciously. With most individuals, what passes for thought is mainly *"drift."* A mere passive reception, and passing along of *"thought currents"* which are unconsciously *"inspired"* and *"respired."*

By the constant "materialisations" of his thoughts, the real thinker, on the other hand, gives proof of the positive character of his thinking, which is merely a foreshadowing of his future. Imagination is the passive phase of the mind's faculty, which, collectively with thought, is rendered as intellect. Unfortunately, owing to the defective *"instruction"* which passes for education, the power of the imagination is restrained almost to the point of atrophy. Little effort, or none at all, is made to stimulate this indifferently comprehended power. In children, the exercise of *"imagination"* is constantly in evidence, but as the wrappings of this outer, gross life of flesh are overlaid, its sensitiveness wanes. *Wordsworth* has finely expressed this in his *"Ode to Immortality."*

It is to the hyper-sensitive mind of him who communes with nature, laying aside the grosser sensation of the physical life, that this *"inner light"* is permitted. In the world of art it rules supreme and absolute. The *"inspiration"* of the musician, the painter or the sculptor, is no more, and no less, than the exercise of a sense which enables them to hear, and see, the "music of the spheres," and the beauties of the "world of visions." To the musician, or to the painter, the theme and the composition are as veritably present "to the eye of the mind" as are the objective realities of the "score" and the "picture" to the normal senses of their beholders. The faculty which art uses to obtain its inspirations is a mere "browsing" in the inner thought-world, a world which in *Occultism* is spoken of as the *Astral Light*.

This *astral light* has been described as "an inner, ambient, penetrative atmosphere, a luminous etheric substance, a natural agent of infinite potency." It is is necessary to the *"psychic"* life of man as atmospheric air is to his physical body. Deprived of either, he becomes "psychically" or "physically" dead. The *astral light* holds in its bosom electric and magnetic forces, and the germs of every conceivable substance. It is this enveloping *"psychic"* thought atmosphere, in which are presented the past, present and future as one eternal, ever-present NOW. We cannot separate, even in thought, cause and effect. The *"present"* is but the result of the "past," and equally so is it true that the "future" is held contained *in potentio* in the "present." When, by the exercise of the imagination, we become cognisant of this vast storehouse, the mind, transcending its material envelope by its own powers, sees, feels and hears, in this sublimated etheric substance, all that it desires.

The individual, who very occasionally is permitted a glimpse into this inner world, is presented under two guises to the physical world. Either as a *"genius"* or a lunatic. In the one case the normal functions of the mind, after its transcendental flight, enable it to express its "impressions" in orderly succession: in the other, mere "babblings" are reproduced, in which the images are distorted and overlaid with the confused "gleanings" in the physical world also. The ultimate "presentations" differ in degree, and arrangement, only.

Eminent psychologists admit how fine is the line which separates genius from insanity. In the case of the genius, it has been inferred that the flights of imagination are occasional only. To this must be added the further limitation that they are rarely made "consciously." That is, the musician, or the painter, does not habitually exercise his will to subdue the normal faculties and open the mind's eye to the "inner light" with a definite purpose. It is more frequently a "casual straying" of the undirected "mind."

Far otherwise is it with the trained clairvoyant. To him, or her, the exercise of the faculty is consciously directed, with set aim, in specific pursuit of knowledge. Although it is generally true that *Clairvoyants*, like painters or poets, are born not made, yet it is essential in each case for the faculty to be trained in its external expression. The child *Mozart* was *"a born musician,"* but his ripened powers, so far as the transcription of the score was concerned, were the results of bringing his normal functions under control, as well as his *"psychic hearing."* So with the *Clairvoyant*. The function of inner vision is the natural outcome of the possession of "etheric senses," which one and all possess in embryo.

In the *Clairvoyant's* case it is an instance of a better "balance" between the objective and the subjective worlds, which is constantly being strengthened by use and exercise. To the senses of the mind *"matter"* is but a shadow, dimly perceived, if at all—the stuff dreams are made of. What to us, with our physical senses, appears as the realm of *"reality,"* is, to the mind, a world of illusion and transitory phenomena, in which "permanence," the only criterion of *"reality,"* is absent. The physical world is essentially one of "change" and not of "permanence." This being so, it will be understood that our three-dimensioned space presents neither difficulty nor obstacle to the inner vision of the clairvoyant. Time in its aspect, to us, of duration, ceases to be. It is merged in the eternal "present."

The *astral light* may further be considered, in the light somewhat of *Haeckel's* "substance," as both *"force"* and *"matter."* In one aspect it is the material of which the inner vehicle of man is formed, his thought body. It is this etheric, fluidic base, upon which, and into which, the outer, denser, "material" particles of the physical body are built. At death, the mind, wrapped for the time being in its astral envelope, passes out of the physical body on to the next plane. This is practically what happens, in a minor degree, in sleep, more completely in the induced sleep of hypnotism, and more fully still in the "suspended animation" of a protracted trance. At death, however, a final separation is made from the physical envelope. The astral vehicle is sometimes seen by clairvoyants as the phantom of the dead, and occasionally by others, whose hyper-sensitiveness to these visions is usually attributed to the "nerves" being out of order. A diagnosis which is defective. For, far from the nerves being out of order, from the occult standpoint, they have reached a condition of "exaltation" which permits for the moment, the inhibition of the normal faculties, and allows a transient glimpse, to the partially awakened inner senses, into another world.

In the deepest *Hypnosis,* when the normal senses are absolutely passive, the inner vision of clairvoyance is abundantly manifested. But the more effectual use of the faculty, and in fact the only one which should be "cultivated," is the consciously directed personal exercise. To do this the physical life must be subdued and subordinated to its proper position. A purified and concentrated "will," dominating a positive "thought-output," will inevitably awaken "reflection," the power of the imagination, the eye of the soul or mind, the inner vision. The faculty, in fact, which is the possession, and distinction, of the clairvoyant.

To follow the analogy hinted at previously, the etheric sense of vision which is exercised in clairvoyance may be likened to the power of the X-rays. Just as these rays penetrate matter, which is normally opaque to ordinary light rays, and are obstructed by substances that are transparent to ordinary light rays, so do the etheric senses in clairvoyance transcend the ordinary limitations of space. A light ray will travel from the remotest star and be visible here on earth. No limitation can be placed upon its capacity to travel so long as a medium exists for its transmission. It becomes visible only when there is something to reflect it. But reflected or not, it travels on through infinite space. Thought possesses a similar capacity: but in other directions also. It can travel through space. It can also travel through time. It can search the boundless past, it can rove throughout the infinite present, it can search the limitless future. No fetters can be placed upon thought. It is coextensive with space, and eternal likewise. Not the thought of an individual thinker. But the thought substance, which, in the individual, is a *"drop,"* isolated for purposes of our examination, or the *"ocean"* of thought.

In this thought ocean, from which we derive our thought substance, the psychoplasms, are stored all the mental experiences, past, present and future. Just as in *Mother Earth* are stored all the possibilities of form and substance of the physical plane. The blade of grass, the elephant, the man, the hero, the *demi-god,* all lie physically present in the womb of *Mother Earth.* The ear of corn, and the man himself, who feeds upon the ear of corn, change places at times. They occupy each the position of the other. The corn becomes the man physically. And the man becomes the corn.

In the eternities, devoid of our illusion of time, the interchange is immediate and present. There is no differentiation. The changes which we perceive taking place in sequence are there seen as an ever-present "Now." This, too, holds good of the etheric realm of thought. Past, present and future may be cognised as the completed and eternal cycle and circle. The present, to us, is merely the shadow of the past, from which it cannot in any way be separated. The future is the extension of the present, with which it is indissolubly bound up.

To this etheric realm, then, the *Clairvoyant* has access. The etheric senses permit the use of the rays which lie beyond the spectrum. Matter which is opaque to the normal vision is transparent to the eyes of the psychic. The walls of a room, the mountain range, a continent or an ocean, oppose no limitations to the traverse of the etheric sense. Like the light ray, it travels on till it strikes the matter it is in search of, and then illuminates it.

So, when the *Clairvoyant* desires to see events which

are happening in distant parts, or to review the past, or to see the future, the grosser senses are laid down and the penetrative rays of the etheric senses brought into action. With the speed of light, space is traversed. Instantaneously, the past or future is surveyed. To effect this transition of consciousness, from one plane of existence to the other, the clairvoyant assumes the trance condition. The normal senses, as in hypnosis, are inhibited. And the mind, freed from its interaction with physical stimuli, reacts to the finer vibrations of the etheric realm. Modern science—psychology—posits the existence of a sub-conscious, or supra-conscious mind. It is this which functions, so it is said, when the normal mind-functions are inhibited. It is this which records, with never-failing accuracy, all that fails normally to impress itself upon the grey substance, to be recovered as ordinary memory.

In *hypnosis,* of the simpler kinds, it is easy to awaken the memory to records of events that have no power to make themselves available under ordinary conditions. In the deep phases of *hypnosis* (this is admitted by the text-books of the *exact* sciences), it is possible to induce a condition in which information is obtained from the clairvoyant. The phenomena of clairvoyance is produced by the regular medical practitioner and a disinterested subject. Far-sight, vision at a distance, and penetration of opaque substances, are exhibited under favourable conditions.

In all this, it is urged there is nothing mysterious. There is nothing which is not clearly traceable to the operation of natural laws. The X-ray will penetrate opaque substances and set up chemical dissociations in photographic materials, though such rays do not behave like ordinary rays, nor do they act as ordinary light rays with regard to our normal vision. It is, therefore, at least possible that in the almost unlimited range of light rays that there are outside our normal vision, there may be, and are, other rays which will react upon the finer, more highly developed senses, the etheric senses, of the clairvoyant.

There can be no real opacity in matter, if matter be, as it is in the last analysis, merely an agglomeration of ether, surcharged with electric force. Eggs will not run through the interstices of an ordinary sieve. But small shot will. Through a sieve with finer apertures flour will pass. And yet we can make a sieve that will hold water. The analogies are rough. But they are intended to shew that our knowledge of the limitations of matter, when we speak of its opacity, is mainly negative. The ordinary attitude is to deny that of which we have no positive knowledge. The telepathist is the Marconi of the occult world. The clairvoyant is merely one step ahead of him.

No one dreams to-day of disputing the fact of *wireless telegraphy*. There are already a large number of people who are convinced, by practical demonstration, of the truth of telepathy as a normal function for those who are willing to attempt to use it. Before long clairvoyance will have established itself also as a practical possibility for most persons. It will then no longer be an occult art except for those to whom the ordinary functions of everyday science are yet a mystery and an indissoluble marvel.

As the great subject of Clairvoyance in its different phases, and especially "Spiritual Clairvoyance" is most fully covered in my late work, namely, Crystal Gazing And Spiritual Clairvoyance, it is unnecessary to print more regarding this subject upon these pages. Let it be understood that Clairvoyance, in all of its different aspects; and especially that phase of it which opens the door into Spirit life, and brings the investigator in touch with the Spirits of the Astral Plane, is a deep and mighty interesting science. Clairvoyance, or general spirit vision, with its different degrees, is taken up most com-

pletely in the above mentioned book, and as the price is a very small one, in comparison to the value of the knowledge contained in the work, any interested student will, without hesitation, obtain a copy. Said book is fully described in Messrs. de Laurence, Scott & Company's great Catalogue Of Occult And Spiritual Books.

CHAPTER XI

SPIRITISM

Many *ancient* peoples preserved traditions of a race of *"divine kings,"* who ruled over them in a golden age, the more definite recollections of which had long since perished. These great rulers, as befitted their implied superhuman origin, were reputed to have possessed command over natural powers to produce effects mysterious and terrifying. As the remembrance of these divine kings faded a priestly class arose who assumed the divine prerogatives. They claimed no divine origin, but were the accredited guardians of a knowledge which conferred power, amongst others, to raise the "spirits" of the dead, and to hold converse with them. These peoples were distinguished by a high degree of evolution, evidenced by an acquaintance-ship with the arts and sciences.

At the opposite pole, in the lowest types of humanity, the same belief in *"spiritual forces"* may be found. The negro of *West Africa*, the *Malay* of *Asia*, and the *Peruvian* of *America*, to say nothing of the *Norseman* of *Europe*, all have legends and practices giving support to universal credence in *"spiritual forces."* The anti-climax is to be found in the adherence of millions to a creed, the essence of which is the belief in the power of *"spirit-raising"* and "post-mortem communion." This is, of course, Spiritualism. The definition Spiritism, though often confused with *Spiritualism* (a less extensive issue), really covers a field of far greater scope, and includes all who profess a belief in the survival and energetic manifestation of the "souls" or "spirits" of gods and men.

As it is proposed to deal here with the possibilities of "spirit-raising" from the scientific standpoint, rather than from that of the "emotional necessity" for survival, it will be well first to clear the ground. We will agree to call the soul of man the sum of those psychic functions which are correlated to "cerebration." The "spirit" the all-embracing energy of motion: the inherent energy which pervades "substance." Ether, the imponderable, space-filling substance, continuous and non-atomic. Matter, the ponderable, atomic mass whose functions are gravity, inertia, molecular motion or heat, and affinity.

So far we are in total agreement with the definitions of Haeckel. It is when we come to consider the fundamental postulates deduced from those propositions that we differ. "Ether is in eternal motion, and the specific motion of ether, whether we conceive it as vibration, strain, condensation, etc., in reciprocal action with mass movement, gravitation, is the ultimate "cause" of all "phenomena." Matter therefore derives its phenomenal appearance from the movement of ether; the energy of which or capacity to do work is the inherent power of "spirit" manifesting as "motion."

Since all phenomena owe their objective reality to the movement of ether, it follows that the "cerebration" of the brain is due to the etheric movement we distinguish as "psychic activity," or the functioning of the soul. It is necessary to emphasise this point, as it is sometimes customary to speak of "force" as a function of "matter." But we cannot conceive of matter (the "product" of the motion of the "ether") being a "source of motion" if it is at the same time held to be a "consequence" of it.

Psychic activity, then, or soul functioning, is another

mode of motion of the ether, one of which is the "materialisation" as objective reality of ordinary "matter." Another "mode" is life, the sum of the determining relative movements associated with the "individuality." The conclusions which we are forced to admit are (1) that matter is merely a transitory form of what, for want of a better name, we term ether; (2) that ether pervades the whole of space; (3) that, in essence, that is in its ultimate aspect or condition, it is infinite in extension and eternal in duration; (4) that ether is ceaselessly in motion; (5) that this eternal motion we may call spirit.

Further consideration shews us that one of the fundamental laws of objective existence is "periodicity." This is a law whose action calls into being, as an "object" for our material senses, all that is. The operation of this law produces our own phenomenal appearances, as personalities, for the brief space of an earth-life. The molecular movements of life (and their chemically allied physiological changes) are due to ether movement, itself the outcome of inherent energy, spirit. The culmination, so far, of etheric movement is seen in "psychic activity," which dominates the mature personality.

Evolution, due to etheric movement, has afforded the fittest vehicle for the manifesting of its potencies, for relatively higher and more complex movements, in the functioning of the human soul as its present climax. Ether and its inherent motion are "eternal," and we cannot therefore admit the idea that, even when the transitory mode of its "objective reality" ceases to manifest, the etheric motion which caused it ceases to be. It cannot cease to be, being eternal.

Matter in its essence, as ether, is eternal, and force or motion is also eternal and inannihilable. Its "mode of manifestation" may, and does, change. But the sum total, whether viewed as the "motion" or the "thing moved," remains constant. Its cessation of functioning in one form or mode necessarily implies its re-emergence as "potential" (passive) or "kinetic" (active) energy in another form or mode. There is no alternative. Persistence of "force" must be postulated for the energy which functions as "psychic activity" as well as for any other mode of motion.

At the moment of physical death such a change of mode occurs. The life motion we regard as "physical," in its relation to chemical and physiological changes in the body itself, changes its mode, from aggregation and association, to segregation and dissociation. The cellular organisation "breaks up." The motion we cognise as "psychic," in relation to its functional activity as the soul, also changes its mode, by withdrawing from the plane of objective reality. It now functions through a less substantial, but still material, vehicle.

All the phenomena of hypnotism substantiate the hypothetical "etheric substratum" body or vehicle. This vehicle is the etheric double, or counterpart, of the physical body, and "persists" for some time as a specific entity after death. It is energised, though faintly only, by the "psychic activity" with which it has been associated during the earth-life of the personality. Its plane of operations is that now spoken of as the "astral," the plane upon which much of our consciousness in "dreams" and "imagination" functions. The power of objective existence, as a materialised personality, has for the moment passed, because the law of "periodicity," which caused its appearance, has now swung back into the period of dissolution.

The persistence of the *astral* vehicle for a time after death, as a partially conscious entity, which, under certain conditions, may give evidence of its actuality, is the basis upon which rests the entire evidence for "spirit" appearances, in séances, apparitions of the

SPIRITISM

dead, or dying, and the other phenomena of spirit-raising and demonology. Leaving aside the fact that many of the occurrences reported have been proved to be a mass of trickery, where professional, *i. e.* paid, assistance has been given, there yet remains a considerable volume of "scientifically accredited evidence" which is explicable only on this thesis of the "persistence of psychic activity" after death.

In most cases of "spirit appearances"—in Spiritualism, for example—the presence of a medium is a necessity. His or her "etheric double" is the material used to produce the "simulated appearances." This plastic, imponderable, fluidic substance is energised by the psychic activity of the medium, and assumes a material presentment. This counterfeiting of another form may be accomplished in two ways. Either the disembodied entity is present and assists to make more "material" the partly discarded astral of the medium, or it may be, and usually is, that the "materialisation" is wholly due to those present at the séance. Thought energy is one of the most potent "forces." It functions principally in the ether, and may act in various ways. In telepathy, by etheric vibration and "conscious cerebration"; passively in clairvoyance, as "imagination," by its perception of movements in the astral light. In Spiritism, by the etheric "strain" it imposes, which then compels a plastic, imponderable fluid to assume, for the time, all the qualities of "matter" and any "form" desired.

That the "return of the dead" is accompanied by any good result, either to the disembodied or the circle, is debateable. The law of periodicity demands a constant change of form and mode. The post-mortem state of the dead is, to them, practically one of rest, for the assimilation of the experiences in earth-life. And interruption of this state must necessarily interfere with the further progress. In normal cases "the disembodied entity" is no more able to assist those who still function on the physical plane, than before decease. This is demonstrated by the fact that no knowledge which was not already accessible, has ever been derived from communion with those passed over. This is as might reasonably have been expected. If the disembodied entities of the dead are at rest, they would be making no definite progress in experience or knowledge. It would be impossible, therefore, to obtain from them any further information than that known to them in their earth-life.

But, if it be admitted, as it must be, that there are many stages in human knowledge: that there are those who have progressed far beyond the ordinary boundaries: that there may have been, and be, those who by cultivation of psychic and etheric senses have had access to the infinite records of the akasa or astral realm, then it would follow that there may be some definite gain in communion with these great souls. Now occultism does not sanction commerce with necromancy properly so called. It holds that only evil can result from holding converse with the disembodied entities of normal individuals who have left this earth-life. Such converse, it is said, can give no benefit to the living individual seeking it, and retards the spiritual emancipation of the disembodied soul.

But, on the other hand, converse with those other exalted spirits, or great souls, whose spiritual knowledge and progress have released them from the necessity of further earth-lives, is of benefit to those desiring and seeking it. But this is not necromancy. It is more closely allied to the spiritual communion which is typified by Christian or other religious ecstasy. It is the spiritual dwelling in the "Chrestos" for the uplifting of the material body to its perfection. The words of the great Teacher in the New Testament are pregnant with meaning for those who view the matter with true insight. In the Old Testament we read that the "raising" by the woman of Endor incurred the divine displeasure. But Enoch walked with God.

It may be considered a far cry from the spiritualised emotionalism of religion to the dicta of modern science. Yet there is a link. The older, narrower views of science are widening to a perception of the finer and higher forces which lie behind our world of gross materiality. Philosophy, the unification of the deductions from the laws of scientific phenomena, recedes daily from its mechanistic conception of the universe. The older concepts pressed to their last stronghold are found to be insufficient and unsatisfactory explanations. Forced upon the reason of man is seen the necessity for a re-grouping, or a restatement, of his more fundamental notions.

Philosophy tends to become more spiritualistic and less materialistic. Motion, or the great breath, which stirs from non-manifestation to manifestation, whether we view it as the evolution of a new solar system from homogeneous fire mist, or whether it be the gradual aggregation of the atoms which form the crystal, is sensed as underlying all transitory forms. Motion is the giver and destroyer of form. It is action and reaction. It is life. It is intellect. It is soul. It is spirit. It is the all in all.

This being so, and there being but change, and no annihilation, in the universe, spirit lies back and beyond the material universe of our physical plane. Our personalities are composite. Man, too, is matter and motion, body, soul and spirit. And his soul, his spirit, is capable of responding to, and communion with, his spiritual peers and spiritual superiors, whether disembodied or embodied. Each plane is being, of manifestation, of consciousness, has its laws, its vehicles. With each change, each ascent to a higher sphere, greater possibilities are opened to man. As he evolves, to use the more classic term of modern science, man realises more of his potentialities. The impossible, heretofore, becomes the possible now.

Thus, with the awakening of his latent etheric senses, new worlds are opened for his conquest. By meditation is opened a way for the development of his higher faculties. As the muscle is trained by exercise, so the etheric faculties can be evoked and strengthened. And when the pupil is ready the master is ready to assist him. *"Knock and it shall be opened to you" is no spiritual parable. It is a statement of plain speech.* For those who desire communion with the great ones, the shining ones, and are willing to prepare themselves, the path is open. But there are many hardships to be undertaken, and to be overcome, before the gateway is passed.

* * * * * * * * * * *

As the subject of Spiritualism together with the proper instruction and methods for development are fully given in my large volume, namely, The Great Book Of Magical Art, Hindu Magic And East Indian Occultism, it is unnecessary to reprint the same here, and those who wish more knowledge on the subject, are referred to this book, as well as The Book Of Death And Hindu Spiritism.

The subject of Hypnotism is fully dwelt upon in my books treating on this subject, all of which will be found listed in Messrs. de Laurence, Scott & Company's great Catalogue of Occult and Spiritual Books. A letter addressed to this firm with a request for a catalogue, will give you full particulars regarding my other works treating on the above mentioned subject.

BIBLE CONTRADICTIONS

CHAPTER XII

IS the Bible the word of God in its entirety? If it were, there would be no errors, no contradictions in it. It would be plain; give direct guidance to the soul seeking to find the Father. Instead of this directness of utterance there is much ambiguity, and in the place of clear statement we find constant contradictions of the most palpable order. I have gathered some of these and placed them in parallel columns for ease of reference. It has not been necessary to strain after effect, or rend sentences from their context, to establish the opposition of many parts of the Bible to many other parts. The utterances are clearly defined, and in many cases absolute commands, given as directly emanating from the Deity.

Everything good.	Everything not good.
And God saw everything that he had made, and behold it was very good. (Gen. i. 31.)	And it repented the Lord that he had made man on the earth. (Gen. vi. 6.)
No man has seen God.	**Moses saw God.**
No man hath seen God at any time. (John i. 18.)	And the Lord spake unto Moses face to face. (Ex. xxxiii. 11.)
All possible with God.	**All not possible.**
With God all things are possible. (Matt. xix. 26.)	And the Lord . . . could not drive out the inhabitants . . . because they had chariots of iron. (Judges i. 19.)
God does not repent.	**God does repent.**
God is not a man that he should lie, neither the son of man that he should repent. (Num. xxiii. 19.)	And God repented of the evil that He had said that he would do. (Jonah iii. 10.)
God no respecter of persons.	**God respects persons.**
There is no respect of persons with God. (Rom. ii. 11.)	Jacob have I loved, but Esau have I hated. (Rom. ix. 13.)

God just. A God of truth and without iniquity. Just and right is he. (Deut. xxxii. 4.)	**God unjust.** It was of the Lord to harden their hearts that . . . he might destroy them utterly. (Jos. xi. 20.)
God hears every prayer. Everyone that asketh receiveth, and he that seeketh findeth. (Matt. vii. 8.)	**God does not hear every prayer.** When ye make many prayers I will not hear. (Is. i. 15.)
God, a God of peace. The God of peace be with you all. (Rom. xv. 33.)	**He is a God of war.** The Lord is a man of war. (Ex. xv. 3.)
The Lord pitiful. The Lord is very pitiful and of tender mercy. (James v. 11.)	**The Lord pitiless.** The Lord shall have no mercy on their fatherless and widows. (Is. ix. 17.)
Mercy everlasting. His mercy endureth for ever. (1 Chron. xvi. 34.)	**Anger everlasting.** Ye have kindled a fire in mine anger which shall burn for ever. (Jer. xvii. 4.)
Fury not in God. Fury is not in me. (Is. xxvii. 4.)	**God furious.** I will cause my fury to rest upon them. (Ezekiel v. 13.)
God is love. God is love. (1 John iv. 8.)	**God is hate.** I will make mine arrows drunk with blood. (Deut. xxxii. 42.)
God will not destroy. Neither will I again smite any more every thing living. (Gen. viii. 21.)	**God will destroy.** I will utterly consume all things . . . saith the Lord. (Zaphaniah i. 2.)
The remnant of Israel shall not do iniquity nor speak lies. (Zeph. iii. 13.)	Compare modern samples.
Children not punished for fathers. The son shall not bear the iniquity of the father. (Ezekiel xviii. 20.)	**Children punished.** I am a jealous God, visiting the iniquities of the fathers upon the children. (Ex. xx. 5.)
Offerings demanded. Thou shalt offer every day a bullock. (Ex. xxix. 36.)	**Offerings rejected.** I delight not in the blood of bullocks. (Is. i. 11.)

BIBLE CONTRADICTIONS

God tempts no man.

Let no man say when he is tempted, I am tempted of God, for God cannot be tempted with evil, neither tempteth he any man. (James i. 13.)

Order not to kill.

He that killeth any man shall surely be put to death. (Lev. xxiv. 17.)

One law for all.

Ye shall have one manner of law, as well for the stranger as for one of your own country. (Lev. xxiv. 22.)

No man has ascended to heaven.

No man hath ascended up to heaven but he that came down from heaven. (John iii. 13.)

No man has heard God.

Ye have neither heard his voice at any time, nor seen his shape. (John v. 37.)

Michal was childless.

Therefore Michal, the daughter of Saul, had no child unto the day of her death. (2 Samuel vi. 23.)

The dead shall arise.

The trumpet shall sound and the dead shall be raised. (1 Cor. xv. 52.)

Judas hanged himself.

(Judas) cast down the pieces of silver in the temple, and departed, and went and hanged himself. (Matt. xxvii. 5.)

All who call shall be saved.

Whosoever shall call upon the name of the Lord shall be saved. (Rom. x. 13.)

Abraham tempted by God.

And it came to pass after these things that God did tempt Abraham. (Gen. xxii. 1.)

Destroyed in name of the Lord.

And Samuel hewed Agag in pieces before the Lord. (1 Samuel xv. 33.)

A different law for strangers.

Unto a stranger thou mayest lend upon usury; but unto thy brother thou shalt not lend upon usury. (Deut. xxiii. 20.)

Elijah did so ascend.

Elijah went up by a whirlwind into heaven. (2 Kings ii. 11.)

Moses heard Him.

Moses spake and God answered him by a voice. (Ex. xix. 19.)

Michal had five sons.

The five sons of Michal, the daughter of Saul. (2 Samuel xxi. 8.)

The dead shall not arise.

He that goeth down to the grave shall come up no more. (Job vii. 9.)

He did not hang himself.

(Judas) purchased a field with the reward of iniquity; and falling headlong, he burst asunder in the midst. (Acts i. 18.)

All who call shall not be saved.

Not everyone that saith unto me, Lord, Lord, shall enter into the kingdom of heaven. (Matt. vii. 21.)

The Lord is merciful.
The Lord is good to all and his tender mercies are over all his works. (Psalm cxlv. 9.)

Is he?
And Joshua did unto them as the Lord bade him. He houghed their horses . . . and smote all the souls that were therein with the edge of the sword. (Joshua xi. 9, 11.)

The law not destroyed.
Think not that I am come to destroy the law. (Matt. v. 17.)

The law destroyed.
Ye are not under the law, but under grace. (Rom. vi. 14.)

Swear not!
Swear not at all. (Matt. v. 34.)

Swear!
He that sweareth in the earth shall swear by the God of truth. (Isaiah lxv. 16.)

Statutes good.
The statutes of the Lord are right. (Psalm xix. 8.)

Statutes bad.
I gave them also statutes that were not good. (Ezekiel xx. 25.)

God wills all to be saved.
Who will have all men to be saved, and to come unto the knowledge of the truth. (1 Timothy ii. 4.)

Causes some to be damned.
God shall send them strong delusion; that they should believe a lie, that they all might be damned who believe not the truth. (2 Thessalonians ii. 11, 12.)

God good.
Good and upright is the Lord. (Psalm xxv. 8.)

God author of evil.
Shall there be evil in a city, and the Lord hath not done it. (Amos iii. 6.)

Do good in public.
Let your light so shine before men that they may see your good works. (Matt. v. 16.)

Do not good in public.
Take heed that ye do not your alms before men, to be seen of them. (Matt. vi. 1.)

Three years famine offered.
So Gad came to David and said unto him: Thus saith the Lord, choose thee either three years famine, or three months to be destroyed before thy foes. (1 Chron. xxi. 11, 12.)

Seven years offered.
So Gad came to David and told him, shall *seven* years of famine come unto thee? etc. (2 Samuel xxiv. 13.)

BIBLE CONTRADICTIONS

Christ's feet anointed.	Christ's head anointed.
Then took Mary a pound of ointment and anointed the feet of Jesus. (John xii. 3.)	There came unto him a woman having an alabaster box of very precious ointment, and poured it on his *head* as he sat at meat. (Matt. xxvi. 7.)

THE COMMANDMENTS.

Thou shalt not make unto thee any graven image. (Ex. xx. 4.)	Thou shalt make two cherubims of gold. (Ex. xxv. 18.)
Honour thy father and thy mother. (Ex. xx. 12.)	And everyone that hath forsaken father or mother shall inherit everlasting life. (Matt. xix. 29.)
Thou shall not kill. (Ex. xx. 13.)	Slay every man his brother, and every man his neighbour. (Ex. xxxii. 27.)
Thou shall not commit adultery. (Ex. xx. 14.)	I will take thy wives before thine eyes, and give them unto thy neighbour. (2 Samuel xii. 11.)
Thou shalt not steal. (Ex. xx. 15.)	Every woman shall borrow of her neighbour jewels of silver and of gold, and ye shall put them upon your sons and upon your daughters. (Ex. iii. 22.)
Thou shalt not bear false witness. (Ex. xx. 16.)	The Lord hath put a lying spirit in the mouth of all these thy prophets. (1 Kings xxii. 23.)
Thou shalt love thy neighbor as thy self. (Lev. xix. 18.)	Now go and smite Amalek and utterly destroy all. (1 Samuel xv. 3.)